Investment Appraisal

Investment Appraisal

Phil Holmes
Department of Economics
University of Durham

INTERNATIONAL THOMSON BUSINESS PRESS
I ⓣ P® An International Thomson Publishing Company

London • Bonn • Boston • Johannesburg • Madrid • Melbourne • Mexico City • New York • Paris
Singapore • Tokyo • Toronto • Albany, NY • Belmont, CA • Cincinnati, OH • Detroit, MI

Investment Appraisal

Copyright ©1998 Phil Holmes

First published by International Thompson Business Press

I(T)P® A division of International Thomson Publishing Inc.
The ITP logo is a trademark under licence

British Library Cataloguing-in-Publication Data
A catalogue record for this book is available from the British Library

First edition 1998
Reprinted 1999

Typeset by J&L Composition Ltd, Filey, North Yorkshire
Printed in Croatia by Zrinski d.d.

ISBN 1-86152-212-6

International Thomson Business Press
Berkshire House
168-173 High Holborn
London WC1V 7AA
UK

http://www.itbp.com

Contents

For my mother and my father, for their encouragement and support over many years

1 AN INTRODUCTION TO THE INVESTMENT DECISION

Introduction

Decision makers at many levels of organizations are frequently confronted with important choices concerning financial aspects of the organization. Increasingly this is the case not only for decision makers in private-sector organizations, but also those within the public sector. Financial decisions and financial planning are central to the success of any business organization. Any operating plan for a business must have alongside it a financial plan which allows implementation of the proposed operational details. For example, an operating plan for a furniture manufacturer may stipulate that 25 three-piece suites of a particular style are to be produced and sold by the business in each month of the coming year. It will also show the materials, machinery and personnel required to undertake this production. Clearly, there are many factors which are important to enable the plan to be carried out, including suitable designs, labour force and marketing. However, financial considerations are vital if the operating plan is to be implemented. If funds are not available in the right amounts and at the right time it will not be possible to purchase the materials needed, employ the required labour force or have suitable machinery for production. Failure to implement an appropriate financial plan will make it necessary for the operating plan of the business to be changed. Thus while business people clearly face many important decisions, some of which will have a considerable bearing on the success or otherwise of the organization for which they work, financial planning and financial decisions are of considerable importance to the organization.

While all aspects of financial management are important to the operational success of the organization, decisions relating to capital investment are arguably the *most* important. When faced with capital investment decisions a choice has to be made between alternatives. For example, it may be that there are three machines which will perform the same function, but which differ in terms of factors such as purchase price, operating life, running costs and breakdown rates. The organization only requires one of these machines and must choose which is the most appropriate investment. Even where there is only one machine which will perform a particular function, the organization always has the alternative of not purchasing that equipment. Failure to make the right choice between alternatives could involve the organization in very substantial additional costs which will affect its profitability.

More specifically, the significance of the investment decision is due to a number of factors:

- capital investments typically account for a large amount of the funds of the organization;
- capital investments will normally have an important impact on the cash flows of the organization in the future. In particular, the investments are likely to generate cash inflows and commit the organization to cash outflows over a number of years;
- the returns from most investments are not known with certainty at the time the investment is undertaken. Thus, there is an element of risk and uncertainty associated with investment decisions;
- once an investment decision is taken it is often not possible to reverse that decision, or at least, it is very costly to do so; and
- the investment decision can have a direct impact on the ability of the organization to meet its goals.

We can see from these points that investment decisions can determine the future of the organization. Given that a poor investment decision may even lead to the survival of the organization being threatened, it is essential that such decisions are made after considerable thought and on the basis of sound principles. In addition, the scale of investment activity each year is vast and investment decisions can, therefore, have a large impact on the economy as a whole. For example, in 1991 the value of net capital expenditure in manufacturing in the UK was £13 billion.

In this book we aim to set out the techniques which are available to aid decision makers faced with investment decisions. In addition, we will consider the problems faced when using these techniques and their limitations. The techniques presented in this book do not guarantee the success of each investment, but they do enable an investment to be undertaken on the basis of an informed decision which has been made in a way which is consistent with the objectives of the organization. In particular, investment appraisal techniques give the decision maker a sound structure for evaluating, ranking and comparing the alternative investment opportunities available. Given the scale of investment activity which is undertaken each year, such a sound structure for assessing alternatives is important.

THE GOALS OF THE ORGANIZATION

In order that a rational choice can be made between alternatives, we need, first of all, to be aware of the objectives of the organization on whose behalf the choice is being made. When considering investment decisions we usually assume that the choice being made is for an organization which is privately owned (either by individuals who run the company on a day-to-day basis or by shareholders) and which exists to benefit its owners, i.e. it is a private firm. This is the assumption which we will adopt in this book. Thus, the techniques considered and the advice given by the adoption of those techniques relate to private-sector organizations. However, with slight modification the techniques discussed here are also suitable for organizations characterized by common ownership and the pursuance of common objectives. Such organizations will also wish to make the best possible use of the resources at their disposal.

In order to provide advice on how decisions should be made we need to understand what the owners or shareholders of a company desire from ownership. For most shareholders the purpose of owning shares is to increase their wealth as a result of ownership. They are willing to give up money at the time they purchase shares or when they forgo dividends that they could receive, in order to (hopefully) receive returns on their money in the future. Thus, firms should assess alternative investment opportunities with the objective of maximizing the wealth of the shareholders. In saying that decisions should be undertaken with *the* objective of maximizing shareholder wealth we are not claiming that this is the only function which firms perform. Clearly, successful companies satisfy consumer wants, they provide employment, they help bring about technological developments and they can provide benefits in terms of sponsoring cultural or sporting events. However, these benefits are only by-products. If decisions are taken which do not satisfy the company shareholders, then those taking the decisions are likely to be replaced. It is the shareholders who have ultimate control of the company and who have the power to choose the management of the company. Management are acting on behalf of shareholders and *should* therefore take all decisions, including capital investment decisions, with their interests in mind.

WHAT IS INVESTMENT?

We have argued that investment decisions should be taken with the aim of maximizing shareholder wealth. Of itself money does not have value. It is the fact that money can be used by shareholders to purchase or consume goods and services which gives money its value. So, it is normal to consider investment in terms of consumption rather than in terms of money.

A definition
An investment can be defined as any act which involves the sacrifice of an immediate and certain level of consumption in exchange for the expectation of an increase in future consumption.

When a shareholder buys shares in a company or forgoes dividend payments which are retained for reinvestment, the shareholder is giving up the opportunity to use that money to consume now. In addition, the shareholder knows precisely how much consumption is being forgone. The shareholder is willing to do this because he or she hopes or expects to obtain higher dividend payments in the future, which will allow an increase in consumption at that point. However, because the outcome of investments is uncertain, the shareholder does not know how much extra consumption they will be able to undertake in the future. Thus, a certainty is being exchanged for an expectation and each and every investment can be considered to be a gamble. Appropriate appraisal of the investment does not prevent it being a gamble. However, it does allow the gamble to be undertaken on the basis of sound information.

Another point which emerges from the above definition of investment is that an investment can be of any size and any duration. For example, the decision on whether to replace a worn nut on a machine is, strictly speaking, an investment. Purchase of the nut requires the use of cash (forgone consumption) and the benefits from the purchase will accrue over a future time period. On the other hand, the building of a modern new factory costing £200 million is also an investment. Indeed, the above definition does not really distinguish between current and capital expenditure, since *all* expenditures by a firm are undertaken with the expectation of future benefits.

This book is concerned with capital expenditure decisions which involve a substantial outlay and which will bring benefits over a relatively long time horizon. Thus the decision to replace a worn nut is not the subject matter of this book. Such a decision is trivial and routine and requires relatively little thought. The techniques considered here relate to investments of a more substantial nature, which do require careful thought and which have important implications for the future prosperity of the business, i.e. strategic investments. Clearly, the size of investments which meet these criteria will vary with the firm. For example, the building of the £200 million factory would require careful thought and would have important implications for the future prosperity of the company. Equally, however, the purchase by a self-employed businesswoman of a new computer costing, say, £7000 could also meet these criteria. In other words, strategic investments will vary in size depending upon the nature and characteristics of the business undertaking the investment.

A final point to emerge from the above definition is that investment does not just relate to purchasing buildings or machines. It is possible to invest in any type of asset. For example, the commitment of money to a research and development (R&D) project or to an advertising campaign is an investment. Similarly, the purchase of Andy Cole for £7 million by Manchester United can be viewed as an investment, as can the purchase of a racehorse or a Government bond. While we might wish to distinguish between investing in real assets (such as land, machinery or footballers) and investing in financial assets (such as stocks and bonds), intrinsically all of these are the same type of action. An investment is being made which requires the forgoing of consumption in exchange for the expectation of higher future consumption. As such all should undergo sensible investment appraisal. While there may be difficulties in identifying the expected benefits associated with some of these investments, the decision maker should try to assess these and consider whether the investment will increase shareholder wealth.

The investment decision making process involves many stages and may require the attention of many individuals and departments within a firm. The stages of the process start with identifying the alternatives to be considered. For example, a company which operates a drawing office for designs may decide that it is time to consider whether to maintain the office in its current form, or to implement changes. It may identify three possibilities: a project based on computer-aided design (CAD); a project which uses both CAD and computer-aided manufacture (CAM); and closing down its internal drawing-office facilities and using externally purchased services.

The second stage of the investment process involves transforming the alternatives identified in the first stage into workable proposals. In other words, the very general ideas identified at the first stage must be defined more specifically by drawing on relevant expertise from both within and outside the company. For example, the needs of the company in relation to design work must be completely specified and the technical possibilities for CAD and for CAD/CAM need to be established. This information is required before any appraisal of the financial terms of the investment alternatives can be undertaken.

Having identified the four possibilities (maintaining the status quo plus the three possible changes) and formulated these into specifically defined projects, the next stage in the investment process involves deciding which to undertake. In order to do this we need to undertake an investment appraisal exercise. Investment appraisal attempts to determine whether the benefits from undertaking an investment are sufficient to warrant the initial expenditure. This means we must identify the cash flows associated with each alternative. Sometimes cash flows are not easy to identify. For example, how would Manchester United evaluate the expected cash flows associated with the purchase of Andy Cole (presumably some consideration could be given to extra ticket sales and sales of merchandise such as strips)? Or how would a company which is considering building a sports and social centre for its employees assess the impact of any improved employee morale and commitment to the company in terms of cash flows? Nonetheless, if a rational choice is to be made then we need to try to quantify such factors. Fortunately, the cash flows associated with most business investments are of a more tangible nature.

The fourth stage in the investment process involves implementing the decision. This will require planning the project, and undertaking any associated building work or purchases. The final stage of the investment process entails reviewing the project and reviewing the decision-making process. This stage allows the firm to learn from its experiences and to try to improve future decision making within the firm. For example, if a company discovers that the building of a new factory took longer than expected, then in future it could undertake a more thoroughgoing assessment of the building time.

Each of these stages in the investment decision-making process is important and each plays an important role in the success of the business. However, the stage which is considered most fully in this book is the third, namely the decision as to which alternative to undertake.

THE ROLE OF INVESTMENT APPRAISAL AND INVESTMENT APPRAISAL TECHNIQUES

When faced with alternative possible courses of action, the outcomes of which are uncertain, a decision maker has to try to make a choice which is consistent with the goals and objectives of the organization on whose behalf the decision is being taken. Decision makers within firms may develop emotional attachments to particular projects or may wish to pursue a project for reasons which are not connected with the objectives of the owners of the firm. Returning to the drawing office example discussed above, a manager may decide to go ahead with CAD and CAM not because it is in the best interests of the owners, but because he or she wishes to be associated with a 'high-tech' company for reasons associated with their own prestige. In addition, given the complexities associated with many of the alternatives, particularly in relation to determining future cash flows, there may be a tendency on the part of decision makers to make a choice without going through a formal appraisal process with its associated information requirements.

The role of investment appraisal is to try to avoid these pitfalls. A formal investment appraisal process is useful in ensuring that relevant and appropriate information is gathered relating to *all* the alternatives. It enables decisions to be taken with clear consideration being given to the objectives of the organization and the desires of owners. Hence, while the process of investment appraisal does not prevent decision makers taking irrational decisions or choosing 'pet' projects, it ensures that they have to consider the consequences of their choice and reduces the possibility of their taking an uninformed or personally motivated decision. The investment appraisal process can, therefore, be seen as an important means for helping to align the interests of shareholders and their appointed representatives in the company.

In this book we will discuss four main investment appraisal techniques which are available to assist the decision maker. We will also examine practical problems which arise in trying to put these techniques to use and methods which are available for addressing these problems. The investment appraisal techniques which will be discussed are a crucial part of the investment appraisal process. They give definite decision advice on whether to go ahead with a particular project or, where a ranking is to be made, which projects to rank most highly. However, we must bear in mind that the techniques only give advice. They should not be used as hard and fast decision rules. The reason for this is quite simple. Investment opportunities are characterized by considerable uncertainty regarding the future cash flows to be received, the operating life of the project undertaken and many other factors. The investment appraisal techniques require cash flow estimates to be used to provide advice. However, the cash flows used are only estimates and may turn out to be wrong. Therefore, while investment appraisal techniques can be used to inform the decision-making process and to provide a framework within which the investment decision can be taken, they should not replace the decision-making process. It is vital that decision makers augment the guidance given by the techniques with the use of judgement, experience and expertise.

THE IDENTIFICATION OF A PROJECT'S CASH FLOWS

All of the techniques to be discussed in later chapters require the input of data relating to project cash flows. As we have stated above, the techniques are trying to identify whether the cash flows associated with the project under consideration are sufficient to warrant the initial expenditure on the project. In practice, identifying the cash flows will not be easy, particularly for projects which involve sophisticated technology or are 'one-offs'. For example, the development of the Concorde aeroplane in the 1970s involved the investment of more than $2 billion by French and British companies. The companies anticipated sales in the region of 300 planes. However, due to problems, such as swiftly rising aviation fuel prices and noise pollution, only 13 planes were sold. More recently, the experience of the building of the Channel Tunnel between the UK and France has highlighted the problems associated with undertaking 'one-off' investments. The costs associated with building the tunnel have been greater than anticipated, as has the time required before it became operational. Clearly, this has implications not only for the expenditure side of the operation, but also the revenue side.

In practice, the investments undertaken by most businesses are less problematic in cash-flow terms than either Concorde or building the Channel Tunnel. Nonetheless, obtaining relevant and reliable cash-flow data remains difficult, largely as a result of uncertainty regarding lead times, level of sales and costs. The problems caused by uncertainty, together with techniques for assisting decision makers faced with these problems are discussed in Chapters 5 and 6. For the time being, we will concentrate on considering the nature of the cash-flow data required for the investment appraisal process.

The old adage 'garbage in, garbage out' holds true for the investment appraisal process. The advice which is given by the investment appraisal process can only be as good as the data on which any calculations are based. A problem arises in that the collection of reliable data is typically costly. For example, a company which is considering launching a new snack food will require estimates of costs of production, monthly sales, etc. Reasonably accurate estimates of the costs of production may be relatively easily available. However, accurate sales forecasts may require detailed market research, costing considerable sums of money. At the stage where the idea for the new product is first considered, it will be inappropriate to incur such costs. Hence, it is likely that rough preliminary estimates will be prepared in the first instance. However, if the project is taken forward with a view to undertaking detailed consideration, then the preliminary estimates will need to be adjusted and refined and detailed market research may now be appropriate. Similarly, as the project proceeds through the investment appraisal process, more detailed engineering, production and financial data will be required.

In addition to having data which is reliable, it is also important that only relevant data is input into investment appraisal calculations. Of particular concern is the need to avoid using cash-flow forecasts based on accounting conventions, such as the allocation of fixed overheads across divisions within a company. Any fixed costs which a company incurs will not be affected by a decision on a potential project. By definition, fixed costs are fixed and will be the same whatever the outcome of the decision relating to the new investment. The cash flows to be included in the appraisal of any investment can be defined as follows:

The relevant net cash flows to be included in any investment appraisal calculations are the marginal or **incremental** receipts and expenditures solely attributable to the commencement of the project.

We should note that this definition makes no reference to the profits of the organization, but focuses on cash flows. This emphasis on cash flows might appear strange given that business people typically view profit as the key measure of the performance of the business. However, while the level of profit gives a good indication of the well-being of a company at a particular time, it gives a snapshot of the performance of the company, rather than reflecting its long-term performance.

We have seen that when considering undertaking investments in capital projects companies are concerned with forgoing consumption (funds) in one time period in exchange for higher expected consumption (funds) in subsequent periods. While profit gives some measure of the potential consumption of the owners of the company, it does not give a completely accurate reflection of this. The reason for this is that profit is an accounting concept which requires a continuous cash flow (resulting from the operation of the business) to be divided up into discrete time periods (accounting years). Indeed, while a particular investment may have a very beneficial effect on the wealth of the shareholders of a company, it may well lead to a reduction in profits in the period when the investment is undertaken, since the company is paying out funds for the investment. Given that shareholders are concerned with increasing their wealth, rather than increasing profits *in any particular year*, profits are an inappropriate concept when undertaking investment appraisal.

The emphasis on cash flows in the above definition also highlights the need to exclude accounting factors such as depreciation. Depreciation is an accounting convention used to spread the cost of an asset over its estimated working life. For example, an asset which is purchased for £520,000, has a working life of 7 years and will have a scrap value at the end of 7 years of £30,000 depreciates at an annual rate of £70,000. However, for the company the cash flow consequences of the purchase of the asset are not £70,000 per year for 7 years. Rather, the company must pay out £520,000 when the asset is purchased and will receive £30,000 when the asset is sold for scrap. It is only these two cash flows which are relevant to the investment appraisal decision. The importance of this distinction will become more obvious when we discuss the significance of the timing of cash flows in the next chapter. In general, however, accounting conventions should not impact upon the figures included in the investment appraisal calculations, except to the extent that they impact upon actual cash flows (for example, through their impact on the level of taxation the company must pay).

In providing a definition of the relevant cash flows to be included in investment appraisal calculations we have placed emphasis on the word 'incremental'. To include any other cash flows in the calculation would bias the results of the investment appraisal and thus may well lead to inappropriate investment advice. An example will help to illustrate this point.

Example

Consider a firm which is currently producing a snack food called 'Yummytummyfilla' (YTF). The product is selling well (despite its name) and a decision has been taken to expand production. However, the current place of manufacture is working at full capacity and it has been decided to build a new factory to produce the extra output. This factory will cost £1.8 million. It is important to note that this decision has already been taken, but that no costs associated with building the new factory have yet been incurred.

The company is now considering producing and launching a new snack food (thankfully, as yet unnamed). To build a factory to produce the new product will cost £1.2 million. However, production of the new product could take place in the same factory as production of the extra YTF if a larger factory costing £2.6 million is built. It is anticipated that the new product will achieve sales of £400,000 per annum, but that as a result of the launch of the new product, sales of YTF will fall by £75,000 per annum from what they otherwise would be.

In deciding whether or not to go ahead with the production and launch of the new product the company must take account of (among other things) the costs of the factory and expected sales. However, it is only *incremental receipts and expenditures* which should be included in the investment appraisal process. Consider, first, the cost of building the factory if the decision is taken to go ahead with the new product and to produce it in the same (large) factory as the expanded production of YTF. Given that the decision has already been taken to build a factory costing £1.8 million, the incremental cost is £800,000 (£2.6 million − £1.8 million). In the investment appraisal calculations this is the figure which should be used. The figure of £1.2 million (the cost of a new factory for production of the new product exclusively) is irrelevant. This figure should not be used, nor should any apportionment of the costs of the two separate factories be used. (For example, there may be a temptation to say that the factory for production of the new product costs 40% of the total for building both factories (£1.2 million out of a total of £3 million) and therefore a figure of £1.04 million (40% of £2.6 million) should be included. However, this does not represent the *incremental* cost.)

Second, consider the sales figures to be included in the appraisal. Since the launch of the new product will lead to a reduction in sales of YTF, the sales figure to be included in any calculation should reflect this. The incremental receipts from launching the new product are £325,000 per annum (£400,000 − £75,000).

This second factor emphasizes the need to view the impact of any investment on the company as a whole, rather than seeing the investment in isolation. The owners are concerned with the company performance, rather than simply the performance of one particular product or division of the company. It is therefore vital that decision makers consider the impact on associated cash flows of any investment decision.

The above example illustrates the need to give careful consideration regarding the figures to be used as inputs to the investment appraisal process. The concept of which figures to use is not difficult. However, the concept may be *different* from the concepts used to determine which figures to include in other areas of the firm's activities (for example, in preparing accounts or in dividing central administration costs between different divisions of the company). The crucial points for the decision maker to remember when undertaking an investment appraisal exercise are, first, to use actual cash flows and, second, only to include incremental receipts and expenditures. If this is done, one of the major pitfalls leading to the production of biased (and, therefore, inappropriate) investment appraisal advice will be overcome.

THE EFFICIENCY OF FINANCIAL MARKETS

This chapter has argued that the goal of private-sector organizations which underlies investment decisions is the maximizing of shareholder wealth. In practice this is achieved by taking decisions which lead to the maximization of firm or share value. The value of a share of a particular company which has its shares listed on the stock exchange depends upon the supply of and demand for those shares. An important question for the decision maker taking financial decisions within a company is 'Does the stock market make a good assessment of the true worth of the company and its shares?' If it does not, then decision makers should take this into account when taking financial decisions. For example, if a company can increase the value of its shares by changing its accounting procedures in a way which has no real impact on the true worth of the company, then decision makers should arguably concentrate on trying to 'fool the market' in this way, rather than pursuing beneficial investments. On the other hand, if financial markets do accurately assess the true worth of a company, then financial managers should not try to manipulate the market price, since the market will see such manipulation for what it is and not overvalue the company. In these circumstances decision makers should concentrate on making investment decisions which add worth to the value of the company. The crucial question is thus 'Do financial markets price shares in a way which reflects the true worth of the company?' If the answer to this question is yes, then financial markets are said to be 'efficient'. If the answer is no, they are 'inefficient'.

For a financial market to be inefficient it would be necessary for the participants in that market either not to have access to reliable information about a company, or to misinterpret or be misled by the information they do have.

Thus, the efficiency of financial markets is primarily concerned with the availability of information in those markets. In particular, for a financial market to be efficient, information about shares traded in that market should be available to market participants at low cost and the share prices should reflect all the relevant information which is available. In practice, there are good reasons why it might be expected that financial markets will not misprice shares. In particular, financial markets are characterized by considerable competition and a good information service. In relation to the competitive nature of financial markets, it is particularly important that there be very many analysts, either investing funds on their own behalf or acting on behalf of other investors. These analysts all operate with the aim of obtaining as high a return as possible on any investments they make. Hence, investment analysts are continually looking for a security that is underpriced in which to invest, and trying to identify overpriced securities to avoid investing in these. In attempting to find under- and overpriced securities analysts gain access to considerable information about the securities and about the prospects for those securities.

Consider, for example, shares in firms such as British Telecom or ICI. It is obvious, even to people who know little about financial markets, that these companies are well known and that there is considerable information available about them. In addition, if important information becomes available about these companies (for example, concerning an investment decision) which affects the true worth of the company, there are many investors who will wish to buy or sell shares rapidly. For example, if an investment is undertaken by ICI which increases the true worth of the company, then people will wish to buy ICI shares before the price rises to reflect the new true worth (the new information). In searching out information about companies, it might be expected that analysts find out all that is relevant to the price of a share and, through their actions, lead share prices to reflect the true worth of the asset. Thus, the intense competition to find underpriced securities and avoid overpriced securities might lead to there being no securities which are in fact over- or underpriced.

If a market is efficient, prices rapidly reflect all available information about the true worth of the company and managers will be unable to fool financial markets into overpricing the shares. When the shares of the company are traded in such a market the decision makers within the company should concentrate on taking investment decisions where the benefits of the investment outweigh the costs of the investment. They should, therefore, avoid wasting time trying to mislead the market and instead try to make sound investment decisions. In practice, financial markets in most developed economies are efficient, at least as far as the vast majority of investors are concerned. There may well be some people with access to inside information which allows them to buy undervalued shares and sell overvalued shares (for example, buying shares on the basis of inside information, before it is announced that a company has signed a major new sales contract). However, such activity is illegal in many countries (such as the UK and the USA) and is not available to the vast majority of investors. Financial managers when taking investment decisions should therefore work on the basis that financial markets accurately price securities.

This chapter has set out a number of issues regarding financial management and the investment appraisal process which are important for the success of a business. It is important that these issues are understood before the techniques to be discussed in later chapters can be sensibly utilized. The key points from this chapter are:

- Financial decisions and financial planning are central to the success of any business organization. Failure to implement an appropriate financial plan will make it necessary for the operating plan of the business to be changed.
- Decisions relating to capital investment are arguably the *most* important because they account for a large portion of the funds of the organization, have an important impact on the future cash flows, are typically characterized by risk and uncertainty, are difficult or very costly to reverse, and have a direct impact on the ability of the organization to meet its goals.
- Investment appraisal techniques enable an investment to be undertaken on the basis of an informed decision which has been made in a way which is consistent with the objectives of the organization. The techniques discussed in later chapters provide a sound structure for evaluating, ranking and comparing the alternative investment opportunities available.
- A rational choice between alternative investments can only be made once the decision maker is aware of the objectives of the organization on whose behalf the choice is being made. In private-sector organizations the assessment of alternative investment opportunities should be undertaken with the objective of maximizing the wealth of shareholders.
- An investment can be defined as any act which involves the sacrifice of an immediate and certain level of consumption in exchange for the expectation of an increase in future consumption.
- The role of investment appraisal is to ensure that relevant and appropriate information is gathered relating to *all* the alternatives and to enable decisions to be taken with clear consideration being given to the objectives of the organization and the desires of owners.
- Investment appraisal techniques can only provide advice to the decision maker. They should not be used as hard-and-fast decision rules, since investments are typically characterized by considerable uncertainty. Decision makers should augment the guidance given by the techniques with the use of judgement, experience and expertise.
- The advice which is given by the investment appraisal process can only be as good as the data on which calculations are based. The relevant net cash flows to be included in any investment appraisal calculations are the incremental receipts and expenditures solely attributable to the commencement of the project.

- A financial market is said to be efficient if all relevant available information about shares traded in that market is fully reflected in share prices. If a market is efficient, prices will reflect the true worth of the company and managers will be unable to fool financial markets into overpricing the shares.
- When the shares of the company are traded in an efficient market the decision makers within the company should concentrate on taking investment decisions where the benefits of the investment outweigh the costs of the investment. They should, therefore, avoid wasting time trying to mislead the market and instead try to make sound investment decisions to meet the goals of the organization.

QUESTIONS

1.1 Why is the investment decision of importance to firms?

1.2 Why do we assume that *the* goal of a private-sector organization is to maximize shareholder wealth?

1.3 Which of the following purchases would normally be considered to be worthy of investment appraisal (explain your answer in each case):

(a) buying a new computer system;

(b) buying software for a computer;

(c) purchasing a photocopier;

(d) purchasing supplies of paper for use in a photocopier;

(e) building an extension to a factory;

(f) refitting the company gym and social club;

(g) undertaking a new advertising campaign?

1.4 What are the main stages of the investment decision-making process?

1.5 Do investment appraisal techniques provide decision makers with decision advice that they definitely should follow? Why or why not?

1.6 To what extent should accounting conventions be included in the investment appraisal process?

1.7 From the point of view of investment appraisal, why does it matter whether or not a financial market prices shares accurately?

2 THE TIME VALUE OF MONEY, DISCOUNTING AND PRESENT VALUES

Introduction

In Chapter 1 we saw that investment decisions should be taken with the objective of maximizing shareholder wealth. It is also evident from the definition given earlier that investments are characterized by the outlay of valuable resources in one period in return for the expectation of more resources being available to the investor in the future. This characteristic leads to the basic problem which is faced when appraising investment opportunities: namely, in trying to meet the objective of maximizing shareholder wealth, the decision maker must make a trade-off between money to be received now and money to be received later. In particular, the decision maker must decide how much money to be received in the future is necessary to compensate the investor for forgoing consumption (money) now. In addition, given that a certain level of consumption is being given up in exchange for an expectation of higher future consumption, the decision maker must make some assessment of the impact of uncertainty on the investment decision. The problems caused by uncertainty and the methods available for dealing with these problems will be addressed in later chapters. In this chapter we will consider the problem of how to trade-off sums of money to be received at different points of time. We will see that it is not only amounts of money to be paid out and received which are important to the investment decision, but also the times at which money is realized. Thus, this chapter introduces the very important concept of the time value of money and shows that in order to make a sensible trade-off between money to be expended or received at different times, we need to have an understanding of the techniques of discounting and compounding.

In order to assist understanding of the concept and the techniques, we will begin by assuming that the sums of money resulting from an investment which are to be received in the future are known with certainty. In addition, we will initially ignore the problems caused by inflation by assuming that the economy in which the decision maker is operating has a zero inflation rate, i.e. £1 today buys the same amount of goods as £1 in the future. These assumptions of certainty and zero inflation are made simply to aid understanding of the issues and will be dropped in later chapters once such an understanding has been gained.

In order to make a sensible trade-off between money to be received at different points of time we need to recognize that money has a time value: that is, a given sum of money has greater value if it is received earlier rather than later. The reason for this is simple: money received earlier can be profitably invested. To illustrate, consider an investor (an owner of, or shareholder in, a company) who is evaluating an investment opportunity which requires an immediate outlay of £1,000 and which will generate income in subsequent years. In deciding whether to go ahead with the investment, the investor will be concerned with how much income will be generated in the future. A rational investor would be unwilling to undertake the investment if they know that they will receive less than £1,000 in income. Let us therefore suppose that the investment will yield a total income of £1,200 in the future. Should the investor go ahead with the investment? At this stage we do not have enough information to answer this question. Two vital pieces of information are missing: the timing of the income, and the rate of interest which could be earned on the £1,000 if it is not invested in this particular investment opportunity. If we assume that the interest rate is 10% and the £1,200 from the investment opportunity is to be received in one year, the investor can now make a rational choice. The investor can either invest £1,000 in this particular opportunity or invest the £1,000 for one year at a rate of interest of 10%. To make a choice, the investor should consider the payoff to be received from investing the money at a rate of interest of 10% and compare this with the £1,200 payoff from the investment opportunity. If the £1,000 is invested at an interest rate of 10% the investor will have £1,100 at the end of the year. This sum is calculated as follows:

$$V_1 = SI(1 + r) = (£1000)(1.1) = £1100 \tag{2.1}$$

where V_1 is the value in one year, SI is the sum invested and r is the rate of interest.

Clearly, in this case the investor would choose the investment opportunity as this yields the larger sum of money. However, if the investor has to wait two years before receiving the £1,200 the investor should choose not to undertake the investment. This is because the £1,000 can be invested at a 10% rate of interest for two years which will yield the following sum of money after this period:

$$V_2 = SI(1 + r)(1 + r) = SI(1 + r)^2 = (£1,000)(1.1)^2 = £1,210 \tag{2.2}$$

where V_2 is the value in two years and all other symbols are as defined earlier.

The example illustrates the importance of the timing of the receipt or expenditure of cash flows and that it is not sufficient to treat money to be received in the future as having the same value as money to be received immediately. Indeed, if the £1,200 resulting from the investment were not to be received for five years, the investor would be much worse off as a result of undertaking the investment opportunity, since by investing £1,000 at 10% rate of interest the investor would have £1,610.51 (this represents the value V_5 calculated as £1,00 $\times$ $(1.1)^5$) at the end of year 5 rather than the £1,200 from the investmen opportunity.

If the decision maker is to be able to make a choice about whether to g ahead with an investment or is to be able to rank investment opportunitie where there is more than one alternative, then a way must be found to allov money to be received at different points of time to be compared. One way c making the comparison is to use the approach adopted above: namely to wor out what the value of money to be received now will be at the point in th future when other money will be realized. The method of calculating V_1, V_2 anc V_5 above can be generalized to find the future value of any sum of money a any point in the future. The formula for calculating future values is:

$$\text{Future value in year } n = V_n = V_0(1 + r)^n \qquad (2.3$$

where V_0 is the value now. In the examples given above V_0 = £1000, r = 10% and V_n was equal to £1,100 for n = 1, £1,210 for n = 2 and £1,610.51 for n = 5 This says that £1,000 now has a future value of £1,100 in one year, £1,210 in twe years and £1,610.51 in five years when the interest rate is 10%. Equation (2.3 can be used to calculate the future value of any sum of money for any interes rate for any time in the future. Thus, for example, the future value of £75 in 2(years when the interest rate is 16% is

$$\text{Future value in year 20 of £75} = V_{20} = £75 \times (1.16)^{20} = £1,459.56 \qquad (2.4$$

PRESENT VALUES AND DISCOUNTING

Future values are a useful concept and help to capture the principle which underlies the time value of money. However, when considering investmen opportunities the decision maker is typically faced with a *stream* of cash inflow: and outflows, rather than just comparing money to be expended now with a single sum of money to be received at some point in the future. So, we need tc convert all cash flows received at different points of time to a common reference point to allow direct comparison.

Consider, for example, an investment which requires the expenditure of £2,000 now and which will generate the following cash inflows over the nex five years (Table 2.1). While it would be possible to convert all the sums of money to the future values for the time period associated with the most distan cash flow resulting from the investment opportunity (i.e. the end of year five), i is easier to think in terms of what future cash flows are worth now, thus using the present time as the common reference point. This simply requires a reversa of the way in which future values were calculated. It was seen earlier that £75 now has a future value in twenty years of £1,459.56 when the interest rate is 16%. It, therefore, follows that £1,459.56 to be received in twenty years time, when the interest rate is 16% has a value now, or a *present value*, of £75. Similarly, £1,610.51 to be received in five years when the rate of interest is 10% has a present value of £1,000. The use of the present time as the common

The Time Value of Money, Discounting and Present Values

Table 2.1

Year	Cash inflow (£)
1	200
2	475
3	600
4	650
5	800

reference point, rather than some future point of time, is particularly useful when comparing projects of different lengths of life. For example, if two projects are to be compared, one which has an expected life of five years (i.e. will generate cash flows for five years) and the other having an expected life of nine years, it is easier to convert cash flows to their present value than to a future value. Comparison at some future point would require conversion to year-nine values for both the five-year project and the nine-year project. In addition, expressing the values of projects at the current time makes the concept more readily understandable.

The present value of a sum of money to be received in the future is calculated by dividing the future sum by $(1 + r)^n$ as follows:

$$\text{Present value} = P = \frac{V_n}{(1 + r)^n}. \tag{2.5}$$

Taking a future sum of money and calculating its present value in this way is known as *discounting*. Equation (2.5) can be used to discount any future sum to its present value and thus allows sums of money to be received at different points in time to be expressed in terms of a common reference point. Returning to the cash flows shown in Table 2.1, we can now discount these to their present values and compare the total of these with the £2,000 required to generate this series of cash flows. Assuming that the interest rate (or discount rate) is 10% then the present value of the cash flows is as shown in Table 2.2.

The total of the five present values is £1,965.87. Thus while the series of cash flows over the five years total £2,725, the present value of these cash flows is less than £1,966. By expressing cash flows in their present value form it is possible to take account of the time value of money and thus to make a direct comparison with the amount required to be invested to generate the cash flows. As the sum of the present values is less than the amount to be invested (£2,000), the investment is not worth undertaking. Undertaking the investment would lead to the investor being £34.13 (£2,000 − £1,965.87) worse off than if the investment were not undertaken. If the decision maker had not taken account of the time value of money and had simply added up the cash flows then he or she may have been misled into undertaking the investment on the grounds that the sum of cash flows is greater than the sum invested. To confirm that undertaking the investment would not be the correct decision we can consider the

Table 2.2

Year n	Cash inflow (£)	Discount by $(1 + r)^n$	Present value (£)
1	200	1.1	181.82
2	475	1.21	392.56
3	600	1.331	450.79
4	650	1.4641	443.96
5	800	1.61051	496.74

cash flows which could be generated by investing the £2,000 in an interest bearing account at the beginning of the five-year period. The investor could then withdraw money equivalent to the cash flows associated with the investment opportunity for each of the five years (£200, £475, £600, £650 and £800 and be left with almost £55, as in Table 2.3. Thus the investor would be better off by £54.97 at the end of year five by not undertaking the investment. This sum has a present value of £34.13 (54.97/1.1^5), the difference between the present value of the income stream from the investment and the amount to be invested.

The example demonstrates that it is essential to take account of the time value of money and to discount future sums to their present value before making a decision on whether a particular investment opportunity is worth pursuing. The concept of the time value of money and the need to discount future cash flows to their present values are of vital importance in considering investment opportunities. It is through the concept of present values that decision makers can make the trade-off between money to be received at different points of time. Crucially, failure to take account of the time value of money may well lead decision makers to make incorrect judgements about the desirability or otherwise of an investment opportunity. The importance of discounting has been understood for many years. For example, in a book published in 1971 Hawkins and Pearce state: 'to virtually all economists the only plausible way to choose between different investments is to use a "discounting" method of appraisal' (p. 15)

Table 2.3

(1) Year	(2) Amount invested at beginning of year (£)	(3) Interest earned at 10% per annum (£)	(4) Total at end of year (£) (2) + (3)	(5) Withdrawal at end of year (£)	(6) Funds available at end of year (£) (4) − (5)
1	2,000	200	2,200	200	2,000
2	2,000	200	2,200	475	1,725
3	1,725	172.5	1,897.5	600	1,297.5
4	1,297.5	129.75	1,427.25	650	777.25
5	777.25	77.725	854.975	800	54.975

There are two techniques based on the principle of discounting which have been developed to enable decision makers to take account of the time value of money when appraising investment opportunities: the net present value (NPV) and the internal rate of return (IRR) methods. Both of these will be set out in Chapter 4 and the advantages and disadvantages of both discussed. However, there are two other areas which are worthy of discussion before going on to set out these techniques. First, there are several short cuts which are available when calculating the discounted value of future sums of money. These will be discussed in the remainder of this chapter. Second, despite the weaknesses of techniques which fail to take account of the time value of money, Chapter 3 will be devoted to a discussion of non-discounting methods of investment appraisal. The reason for this is simple. While it has long been recognized that money has a time value and that discounting is essential if incorrect decisions are not to be taken (see the quote from Hawkins and Pearce above), many firms continue to use non-discounting techniques in appraising investments. For example, Sangster (1993) found that while 73% of firms in his study of large companies in Scotland used discounting techniques of appraisal, 78% used the main non-discounting technique (the payback method) and 31% the other major non-discounting technique (the accounting rate of return method). Indeed, Sangster found payback to be the most popular method of investment appraisal used and the figures suggest that over a quarter of all large companies in the study did not use discounting techniques when appraising investment opportunities. Given the continued widespread use of non-discounting techniques it is desirable to have an understanding of these methods and to understand their shortcomings.

ORT CUTS IN DISCOUNTING: ANNUITIES AND PERPETUITIES

We have seen that to calculate the present value of an amount of money, V, to be received n years in the future when the discount (or interest) rate is r, all that is required is to divide V by $(1 + r)^n$. However, we have also seen that in practice the decision maker is typically faced with a *stream* of cash inflows and outflows, and we need, therefore, to convert all sums in that stream to their present values. The sum of these present values is given by amending equation (2.5) as follows:

$$\text{Sum of present values} = \text{SP} = \sum_{i=1}^{i=n} \frac{V_i}{(1 + r)^i} = \frac{V_1}{(1 + r)} + \frac{V_2}{(1 + r)^2} + \frac{V_3}{(1 + r)^3} + \ldots + \frac{V_n}{(1 + r)^n} \quad (2.6)$$

where Σ is a symbol representing the instruction to sum all V_i from the first, V_1 ($i = 1$), to the nth, V_n ($i = n$). As was seen from the example above, the desirability of an investment opportunity is determined by comparing SP with the sum to be invested. If SP is greater than the sum to be invested the investment opportunity is worth pursuing. If SP is less than the sum to be invested, it is not worth pursuing.

Calculation of SP can be made by determining each value of P separately as in equation (2.5) and then adding these together. However, in situations where cash flows are of equal amounts at regular intervals (for example where the income from an investment is £100 each year), the calculation of SP can be simplified. Two regular patterns can be considered which allow use of simplifying formulae: *perpetuities* and *annuities*. We will consider these in order.

Perpetuities

A perpetuity is simply a series of cash flows of a constant amount that goes on perpetually, or for ever. In this case, n in equation (2.6) is equal to infinity. Surprisingly, it is easy to determine a value for such a series of cash flows. The present value of a perpetuity which has the first cash flow one period (say, one year) from now is equal to the value of the constant cash flow divided by the period discount rate,[1] r:

$$\text{Present value of a perpetuity} = \frac{V}{r}. \tag{2.7}$$

Thus, if a regular perpetual cash flow of £100 is to be received and the discount rate is 8%, then the present value of this series is £1,250 (calculated as £100/0.08). An example of a perpetuity is a Government bond which has no redemption date. It promises to pay the holder a fixed amount in perpetuity.

Annuities

An annuity is very similar to a perpetuity, except that rather than the series of constant cash flows being paid in perpetuity, the series has a limited life. Thus, an annuity is a series of cash flows of a constant amount that goes on for a limited period of time, say 20 years. Again, there is a formula which enables the present value of this series of cash flows to be calculated, although the formula is more complex than the formula for the present value of a perpetuity. For this reason it is often better to use discount tables to calculate the present value of an annuity. Discount tables are discussed in the next section. For now, let us consider the formula for calculating the present value of an annuity:

$$\text{Present value of an annuity} = V \left[\frac{1}{r} - \frac{1}{r(1 + r)^n} \right]. \tag{2.8}$$

Thus if a regular cash flow of £100 is to be received each year for the next twenty years and the discount rate is 12%, then the present value of this series is

$$PA = 100 \left[\frac{1}{0.12} - \frac{1}{0.12(1 + 0.12)^{20}} \right] = 746.944. \tag{2.9}$$

Thus while the total amount to be received over the twenty years is £2,000 (20 × £100), the present value of this stream is only £747 approximately.

The present value of an annuity or some other stream of cash flows is relatively easy to calculate using the formulae given above if you have access to a computer or a programmable calculator. However, in the absence of such aids, it is sometimes easier to calculate present values with the use of discount tables. Two tables are of particular use: the present value of £1 table (Table A at the end of the book) and the present value of an annuity of £1 table (Table B at the end of the book). The use of the tables is relatively straightforward. Consider first Table A. Along the top of the table are different discount rates. Down the left-hand side of the table is the number of periods (years). The main body of the table gives present values of £1 for different discount rates and different periods. For example, if the time period in which money is to be received (or paid out) is year 9 (i.e. in 9 years' time) and the discount rate is 8%, then by consulting the cell which corresponds to period 9 and a discount rate of 8% we discover that the present value is £0.50025. This means that £1 to be received in 9 years' time when the discount rate is 8% has a present value of just over 50p. This table can be used to discover the present value of £1 to be received at any future period and for any discount rate given in the table. Thus, £1 to be received in 20 years when the discount rate is 12% has a present value of £0.10367. By using the table we can then calculate the present value of any sum to be received. For example, if £35 is to be received in 9 years and the discount rate is 8%, we simply read the value of 0.50025 from the table and multiply this by 35 to get the present value of £17.50875. The figures in the body of the table (such as 0.50025 and 0.10367) are known as 'discount factors'. The discount factors can be used to calculate the present values of the sums which were shown in Table 2.2 (see Table 2.4).

The use of the table in this case is much easier than calculating the value of, for example, 1.1^5 if you only have a fairly basic calculator. In this example the calculations are exactly the same as in Table 2.2. However, because the discount factors are only approximations (to 5 decimal places) there can sometimes be minor differences in the results between using the tables and calculating the numbers precisely by calculator. However, the differences are very small in most cases.

Table 2.4

(1) Year n	(2) Cash inflow (£)	(3) Discount factor (10%)	(4) value (£) (2 × 3)
1	200	0.90909	181.82
2	475	0.82645	392.56
3	600	0.75131	450.79
4	650	0.68301	443.96
5	800	0.62092	496.74

Table B is similar in layout to Table A and is used in exactly the same way. In this case, however, the figures in the body of the table relate to the present value of an annuity of £1. For example, consider an annuity of £1 to be received each year for 9 years when the discount rate is 8%. This stream of 9 payments of £1 has a present value of £6.24688. Similarly, an annuity of £1 to be received each year for 20 years when the discount rate is 12% has a present value of £7.46944. To find the present value of an annuity for any other sum the discount factor is multiplied by the sum to be received each year. For instance, the example given above for the annuity short cut was for a sum of £100 to be received for 20 years when the discount rate is 12%. By taking the discount factor of 7.46944 and multiplying this by 100, the present value of £746.944 can be calculated. Clearly the use of the table is much easier than the use of equation (2.8) above.

SUMMARY AND KEY POINTS

This chapter has discussed the vitally important issues of the time value of money and the need to discount sums of money to their present values if investment decisions are to be made in a manner which is consistent with the aim of maximizing shareholder wealth. The key points to arise in this chapter are as follows:

- In trying to meet the objective of maximizing shareholder wealth, the decision maker must make a trade-off between money to be received now and money to be received later.
- It is not only amounts of money to be paid out and received which are important to the investment decision, but also the times at which money is realized.
- Money has a time value: a given sum of money has greater value if it is received earlier rather than later since money received earlier can be profitably invested.
- When considering investment opportunities the decision maker is typically faced with a *stream* of cash inflows and outflows. It is therefore necessary to convert all cash flows received at different points of time to a common reference point to allow direct comparison.
- By expressing cash flows in their present-value form it is possible to take account of the time value of money and thus to make a direct comparison with the amount required to be invested to generate the cash flows.
- It is essential to take account of the time value of money and to discount future sums to their present value before making a decision on whether a particular investment opportunity is worth pursuing.
- The concept of the time value of money and the need to discount future cash flows to their present values are of vital importance in considering investment opportunities. It is through the concept of present values that decision makers can make the trade-off between money to be received at different points of time.
- There are two techniques based on the principle of discounting which have

The Time Value of Money, Discounting and Present Values

been developed to enable decision makers to take account of the time value of money when appraising investment opportunities: the net present value (NPV) and the internal rate of return (IRR) methods.

- A perpetuity is simply a series of cash flows of a constant amount that goes on perpetually, or for ever. The present value of a perpetuity which has the first cash flow one year from now is equal to the value of the constant cash flow divided by the period discount rate, r.
- An annuity is a series of cash flows of a constant amount that goes on for a limited period of time, say 20 years. Present value of an annuity tables are available to assist in calculating the present value of such an income stream.

APPENDIX: THE DERIVATION OF FORMULAE USED IN CHAPTER 2

Derivation of equation (2.7): present value of perpetuities

The present value of a perpetuity can be represented as:

$$\text{Present value of a perpetuity} = PP = \sum_{i=1}^{i=\infty} \frac{V_i}{(1+r)^i} = \frac{V}{(1+r)} + \frac{V}{(1+r)^2} + \frac{V}{(1+r)^3} + \ldots \tag{2.A1}$$

Let $V/(1+r) = a$ and $1/(1+r) = x$. Equation (2.A1) can then be rewritten as:

$$PP = a(1 + x + x^2 + x^3 + \ldots). \tag{2.A2}$$

If we now multiply both sides by x we get:

$$xPP = a(x + x^2 + x^3 + x^4 + \ldots). \tag{2.A3}$$

We now subtract equation (2.A3) from equation (2.A2):

$$PP - xPP = PP(1 - x) = a(1 + x + x^2 + x^3 + x^4 + \ldots) - [a(x + x^2 + x^3 + x^4 + \ldots)] = a. \tag{2.A4}$$

Substituting into equation (2.A4) for a and x and multiplying both sides by $1 + r$: Substituting for a and x in equation (2.A4) gives:

$$PP\left[1 - \frac{1}{(1+r)}\right] = \frac{V}{(1+r)}.$$

Multiplying both sides by $(1 + r)$:

$$PP\left[(1+r) - \frac{(1+r)}{(1+r)}\right] = V.$$

Rearranging this equation gives:

$$PP[(1+r) - 1] = PP.\ r = V.$$

and thus,

$$PP = \frac{V}{r}. \tag{2.A5}$$

Equation (2.A5) is the same as equation (2.7) in the main text.

Derivation of equation (2.8): present value of annuities

The present value of an annuity can be represented as:

$$PA = \frac{V}{(1 + r)} + \frac{V}{(1 + r)^2} + \frac{V}{(1 + r)^3} + \ldots + \frac{V}{(1 + r)^n} . \qquad (2.A6)$$

Multiplying both sides by $1/(1 + r)$ yields:

$$\frac{PA}{(1 + r)} = \frac{V}{(1 + r)^2} + \frac{V}{(1 + r)^3} + \ldots + \frac{V}{(1 + r)^n} + \frac{V}{(1 + r)^{n+1}} . \qquad (2.A7)$$

By subtracting equation (2.A7) from equation (2.A6) we get the following:

$$PA - \frac{PA}{(1 + r)} = \frac{V}{(1 + r)} - \frac{V}{(1 + r)^{n+1}} .$$

Multiplying both sides by $(1 + r)$ gives:

$$PA(1 + r) - PA = V - \frac{V}{(1 + r)^n} .$$

Thus:

$$PAr = V\left[1 - \frac{1}{(1 + r)^n} \right] .$$

and rearranging gives

$$PA = V\left[\frac{1}{r} - \frac{1}{r(1 + r)^n} \right] . \qquad (2.A8)$$

Equation (2.A8) is the same as equation (2.8) in the main text.

WORKED EXAMPLES

2.1 Use discount tables to show the present value of the following sums of money:

    (a) £100 to be received in 10 years when the discount rate is 12%,
    (b) £300 to be received in 17 years when the discount rate is 8%,
    (c) £4,500 to be received in 6 years when the discount rate is 18%,
    (d) £3,250 to be received in 11 years when the discount rate is 6%.

Answers:

(a) From Table A we can see that the discount factor for a payment to be received in 10 years' time when the discount rate is 12% is 0.32197. Thus, the value of £1 to be received in 10 years when the discount rate is 12% is £0.32197. The value of £100 to be received at that time, given the 12% discount rate, is £32.197.

(b) From Table A we can see that the discount factor for a payment to be received in 17 years' time when the discount rate is 8% is 0.27027. Thus, the value of £1 to be received in 17 years when the discount rate is 8% is £0.27027. The value of £300 to be received at that time, given the 8% discount rate, is £81.081.

(c) From Table A we can see that the discount factor for a payment to be received in 6 years' time when the discount rate is 18% is 0.37043. The value of £4,500 to be received at that time, given the 18% discount rate, is £1,666.935.

(d) From Table A we can see that the appropriate discount factor is 0.52679. The value of £3,250 to be received in 11 years, given the 6% discount rate, is £1,712.0675.

2.2 A company has the opportunity to undertake an investment costing £9,000 which will generate net cash flows in each of the next seven years of £2,000. Use discount tables to calculate the present value of the future cash flows:

(a) when the discount rate is 8%,
(b) when the discount rate is 12%,
(c) when the discount rate is 20%.

In each case state whether the investment is worthwhile.

Answers:

(a) From Table B we can see that the discount factor for an annuity of £1 for seven years, when the discount rate is 8%, is 5.20636. Thus, the present value of the income stream is £2,000 × 5.20636 = £10,412.72. As this is greater than the cost of the investment, the opportunity is worth undertaking.

(b) From Table B we can see that the discount factor for an annuity of £1 for seven years, when the discount rate is 12%, is 4.56376. Thus, the present value of the income stream is £2,000 × 4.56376 = £9,127.52. As this is greater than the cost of the investment, the opportunity is worth undertaking.

(c) From Table B we can see that the discount factor for an annuity of £1 for seven years, when the discount rate is 20%, is 3.60459. Thus, the present value of the income stream is £2,000 × 3.60459 = £7,209.18. As this is less than the cost of the investment, the opportunity is not worth undertaking.

2.3 What is the present value of a perpetuity of £250 per annum when the discount rate is:

(a) 10%,
(b) 17%,
(c) 23%.

Answers:

The present value of a perpetuity (PVP) is calculated as V/r, where V is the value of the annual cash flow and r is the discount rate. Therefore, the present values for each of the discount rates are as follows:

(a) PVP = 250/0.1 = £2,500,
(b) PVP = 250/0.17 = £1,470.59,
(c) PVP = 250/0.23 = £1,086.96.

QUESTIONS

2.1 What is meant by the term 'the time value of money' and why is it important?

2.2 Why is the concept of the present value superior to that of the future value for comparing investment opportunities?

2.3 Show the formula for calculating (a) the future value of a sum of money and (b) the present value of a sum of money.

2.4 Explain why investments which generate cash flows with a present value greater than the cost of the investment are worth undertaking.

2.5 Why is it important to be aware of the non-discounting techniques of investment appraisal?

NOTE

1 It is not necessary to understand how this formula is derived. However, for those who are interested, the derivation of this formula and that for the present value of an annuity are shown in the appendix to this chapter.

3 NON-DISCOUNTING TECHNIQUES OF INVESTMENT APPRAISAL

Introduction

If criteria consistent with the goals of the organization are to be employed for investment appraisal, we must take account of the time value of money. As we have seen, the need to do this and to discount sums of money to their present values has long been established. However, in spite of the well-known superiority of discounting techniques of investment appraisal, firms continue to use non-discounting techniques to appraise investment opportunities, as was seen from the work of Sangster (1993), discussed in Chapter 2. For that reason it is important to have an understanding of the non-discounting (or traditional) techniques of investment appraisal and, importantly, of the problems associated with these techniques. In particular, it is desirable to have an understanding of why the use of non-discounting techniques may lead to investment decisions being taken which are not consistent with the objectives of the owners of the organization.

In this chapter we will discuss the two most widely used of the non-discounting techniques: namely, the payback method and the accounting rate of return method (also known as the 'return on capital employed' method (ROCE) and the 'return on investment' method (ROI)). Given the unequivocal statement in the last chapter that discounting techniques are the only means of investment appraisal consistent with the goals of the organization, it is perhaps surprising that the non-discounting techniques continue to be widely used. The reason for this is quite simple: inertia.

The discounting techniques of investment appraisal only began to gain acceptance in the 1950s. The payback and accounting rate of return methods have a history of use which predates by many years the use of discounting techniques. As the use of the traditional techniques was established practice in many organizations and as this practice has been handed down from one generation of decision makers to the next, it is a slow process to change to the more widespread use of discounting techniques. The traditional techniques also have the claimed advantage of being easier to understand than are discounting techniques. In practice this so-called 'advantage' is nothing of the sort, since it perpetuates the use of inappropriate methods for appraising investments. A further problem arises from the fact that the traditional techniques of investment appraisal are believed by some to possess superior properties to the discounting techniques in some respects, particularly in relation to the reduction of risk. These beliefs are largely misguided, as will be demonstrated in this chapter. In order to challenge the inertia and tradition associated with the use of the payback and accounting rate of return approaches, it is necessary to understand their shortcomings.

THE PAYBACK METHOD OF INVESTMENT APPRAISAL

As was explained in Chapter 1, all investment appraisal techniques are seeking to identify whether the cash flows resulting from an investment are sufficient to make the investment worthwhile. The payback method adopts the most straightforward approach to this problem. It simply seeks to measure the length of time that will be taken before the receipts from the investment are sufficient to 'pay back' the cost of the investment. The receipts from the investment are measured as the net cash flows resulting from the project being undertaken (i.e. the difference between the total amount of cash receipts and the total amount of cash outlays in each period). To illustrate the use of the payback method consider two potential investment projects which each cost £50,000 and which have the net cash flows as shown in Table 3.1.

Examination of the net cash flows of the two projects tells us that the initial outlay of £50,000 is recouped in 4 years for project A and in five years for project B. Thus project A has a payback period of 4 years and project B has a payback period of 5 years.

The payback method can be used in two ways: first, where projects are independent (i.e. both A and B could be undertaken if they satisfy the investment criteria) the payback method can be used to make accept-or-reject decisions; second, it can be used to rank projects where the investments are

Table 3.1

Year	Project A cash flows (£)	Project B cash flows (£)
1	7,500	10,000
2	20,000	10,000
3	15,000	10,000
4	7,500	10,000
5	3,000	10,000
6	0	10,000
7	0	10,000
8	0	10,000
9	0	10,000
10	0	10,000

Non-Discounting Techniques of Investment Appraisal

mutually exclusive (i.e. either project A will be undertaken or project B will be undertaken, but not both). To use payback in the first way it is necessary first to establish a payback period within which all acceptable projects must recoup the outlay of the investment. The choice of the 'acceptable' payback period is arbitrary, but can be chosen to meet the characteristics of the business. For example, a business with considerable potential cash-flow problems and severe capital rationing may opt for a short payback period, say 3 years. In this case neither project A nor project B would be acceptable to the company. In contrast if a four-year payback period is chosen project A would be acceptable, but B would not be, while a five-year payback period would make both projects acceptable to the company. To use the payback to rank mutually exclusive projects simply requires choosing the project which has the shortest payback period. In the above example this would lead to a choice of project A. The company would then proceed with this project, providing that it meets the acceptable payback period criterion.

As can be seen from this example, the use of payback is very simple and the interpretation of the outcome of assessment of investments using this technique (if that is not too grand a title for such a simple approach) is straightforward. However, the payback period method has a number of shortcomings which make its use highly undesirable, except, perhaps, as an initial screening mechanism in situations where cash-flow problems and capital rationing make early recoupment of capital of paramount importance. From the discussion in the last chapter it is perhaps obvious that the most important shortcoming is that with the payback method no account is taken of the time value of money. However, this can be overcome to some extent by using discounted payback. In this situation the cash flows are discounted to their present value before payback periods are calculated. For example, consider again the cash flows in Table 3.1, but let the cash flows be discounted by the discount factor, assuming the discount rate is 10%. The appropriate figures are shown in Table 3.2 (figures have been rounded to the nearest pound).

Table 3.2

Year	10% discount factor	Project A cash flow	Project A discounted cash flow	Project B cash flow	Project B discounted cash flow
1	0.90909	7,500	6,818	10,000	9,091
2	0.82645	20,000	16,529	10,000	8,265
3	0.75132	15,000	11,270	10,000	7,513
4	0.68301	7,500	5,123	10,000	6,830
5	0.62092	3,000	1,863	10,000	6,209
6	0.56447	0	0	10,000	5,645
7	0.51316	0	0	10,000	5,132
8	0.46651	0	0	10,000	4,665
9	0.42410	0	0	10,000	4,241
10	0.38554	0	0	10,000	3,855

The discounting of the cash flows has a major impact in this case, illustrating the importance of taking account of the time value of money and the severe problems of using payback in its simplest form. First, once the cash flows are discounted project A no longer repays the outlay of the project. The total discounted cash inflows amount to only £41,603. Similarly, while project B does recoup the capital outlay using discounted figures and thus is seen to be preferable to project A, the payback period is considerably longer than for the non-discounted figures at 8 years. Using a payback 'acceptance period' of, say, 5 years would lead to rejection of this project also. However, while discounting the cash flows does make the approach more acceptable, problems remain. Indeed, one of the great advantages which is claimed for the payback method, namely its simplicity, is lost as soon as a discounted payback approach is used. If discounted figures are going to be used why not go all the way and use either of the techniques to be discussed in the next chapter (NPV or IRR)?

The major problems with payback (ignoring the time-value-of-money problem) are that the choice of the payback period is arbitrary and that it only considers cash flows in the payback period (the cut-off point for acceptable projects). Let us consider these two points in more detail. There are no set rules for choosing the length of the payback period for acceptable projects. While some guidance may be given by the cash-flow situation of the company, at the end of the day the choice of the payback period is arbitrary. This can lead to arbitrary decisions about the acceptability or otherwise of projects. For example, project A shown in Table 3.1 above would be acceptable with a payback acceptance period of 4 years or more, but not with a payback acceptance period of 3 years. A technique which leads to decisions being made on such an arbitrary basis and without consideration of the objectives of the organization is not reliable. For example, managers may alter payback acceptance periods from one project to the next to 'justify' making choices which they wish to make rather than which are in the best interests of the owners.

To illustrate the problems associated with not taking account of cash inflows after the payback period consider again the example shown in Table 3.1 on the basis that A and B are mutually exclusive. Using the simple (non-discounted) payback approach project A is preferable to project B, since A has the shorter payback period. However, while A 'pays back' earlier, the cash inflows after the payback period are very different for the two projects. Project A only has cash inflows for a year after the payback period and the inflow is very small (£3,000 in year 5), whereas project B continues to have cash inflows of £10,000 in each year up to and including year 10. Thus, project B generates total returns of £100,000 compared to only £53,000 for project A. This example illustrates a key feature of payback. The payback approach is inherently short-termist and discriminates against those projects which have long lives. Instead, projects which generate returns rapidly are preferred, even in circumstances where those returns are for a relatively short period of time.

Proponents of payback argue that it has two major advantages over the discounting techniques of investment appraisal. First, it is simple to use and to understand. While simplicity is desirable, it should not be *the* determining factor for selecting an appraisal method for choosing between alternatives.

The operation of a typewriter is easier to understand than is the operation of a computer with a word-processing package, but that does not make the typewriter preferable. The second claimed advantage is that payback provides an in-built safeguard against undertaking risky projects. The idea behind this argument is that cash inflows further into the future are inherently more uncertain than are cash inflows in the near future. The payback method concentrates attention on early cash inflows and requires that projects pay back within a short period of, say, 3 or 4 years. The logic of this, according to supporters of payback, is that risky projects are avoided and the risk of making a loss is minimized. For example, if a new product is launched which has a payback period of 3 years, it is possible that it will take competitors that long to respond to the new product in terms of undertaking research, designing a competing product, building a factory, setting up production and marketing the product. Thus, it is argued, the risk of loss is minimized.

The problem with this argument is that far from leading to a reduction in risk, using payback, particularly with a short payback acceptance period (say, 3 years), may well lead to an increase in risk. With a four-year payback period, any acceptable project must yield an average return of 25%, while a three-year payback period requires a 33% average return. Typically, higher returns are associated with riskier projects: few projects which can be considered to be relatively riskless will offer a 33% return. Thus, by demanding rapid payback, companies are building in a bias towards the acceptance of risky projects.

In terms of meeting the objectives of the organization appraising investments, the problems associated with the payback method make it likely that there will be under-investment, with many projects which would increase owner wealth being rejected. This situation arises because no account is taken of the cost of funds. For example, using a four-year payback period, an investment offering an average 20% return would be rejected since this would take 5 years to pay back. This project would be rejected even if funds were available at a cost of 10%. Clearly, if I can borrow funds at 10% and invest them so that I receive a 20% return, my wealth has been increased. The same argument holds true for companies and the owners of those companies. Yet payback would not accept such an investment. Thus while payback may be of use in very particular circumstances and as an initial screening device, it is not a sensible means by which to make investment decisions, since it is not consistent with the goals of the organization.

THE ACCOUNTING RATE OF RETURN METHOD OF INVESTMENT APPRAISAL

As the name suggests, the accounting rate of return (or ROCE or ROI) method is based on the accounting concepts of accounting profit and average capital employed. While it has the advantage over the payback method that it takes account of profits over the whole life of the project, it suffers from a number of shortcomings, not the least of which is that there are numerous definitions for accounting profit and capital employed. Before proceeding to discuss these problems, the method will be set out.

3.1 You are faced with two investment opportunities which each cost £30,⬤
and which have the net cash inflows shown in the table.

Year	Project A cash flows (£)	Project B cash flows (£)
1	7,500	5,000
2	7,500	5,000
3	7,500	6,000
4	7,500	6,000
5	5,000	8,000
6	0	15,000
7	0	15,000

(a) Use the payback method to choose between the two projects, assu⬤
ing a payback period of 4 years.

(b) Using a discount rate of 12%, which project has the faster paybac⬤

Answers:

(a) The payback period for A is 4 years, while that for B is 5 years. Therefo⬤
project A is preferred when payback is used.

(b) With a discount rate of 12%, the discounted cash flows are as shown in t⬤
table.

Year	12% discount factor	Project A cash flow	Project A discounted cash flow	Project B cash flow	Project B discounted cash flow
1	0.89286	7,500	6,696	5,000	4,464
2	0.79700	7,500	5,979	5,000	3,986
3	0.71178	7,500	5,338	6,000	4,271
4	0.63552	7,500	4,766	6,000	3,813
5	0.56743	5,000	2,837	8,000	4,539
6	0.50663	0	0	15,000	7,599
7	0.45235	0	0	15,000	6,785

The total value of the discounted cash flows for project A is £25,61⬤
Therefore, project A does not pay back the initial cash outflow when th⬤
cash inflows are discounted. For project B the total value of the discounte⬤
cash flows after 6 years is £28,672. After 7 years the figure is £35,45⬤
Therefore, using discounted payback, the payback period is approxi⬤
mately $6\frac{1}{4}$ years (assuming the cash flow in year 7 is spread evenl⬤
throughout the year). Thus, project B has the quicker payback perio⬤
when discounted payback is used.

3.2 You are required to choose between two mutually exclusive investments on the basis of the accounting rate of return approach. Project C requires an initial capital outlay of £60,000 and lasts for 6 years, and the expected scrap value after 6 years is zero. Project D requires an initial capital outlay of £10,000 and lasts for 3 years, and the expected scrap value after 4 years is £2,000. The estimated accounting profit (after depreciation) for the two projects is as shown in the table.

Year	Project C – accounting profit £s	Project D – accounting profit £s
1	2,000	1,000
2	4,000	2,000
3	6,000	3,000
4	10,000	
5	11,000	
6	12,000	

$$\text{Average capital employed} = \frac{\text{Intial cost of investment} + \text{Scrap value of investment}}{2}.$$

For project C = (60,000 + 0)/2 = 30,000.
For project D = (10,000 + 2,000)/2 = 6,000.
Average profits:
For project C = (2,000 + 4,000 + 6,000 + 10,000 + 11,0000 + 12,000)/6 = £7,500.
For project D = (1,000 + 2,000 + 3,000)/3 = £2,000.
Therefore, the accounting rate of return for the two projects is:
For C: 7,500/30,000 = 0.25 or 25%.
For D: 2,000/6,000 = 0.333 or 33.3%.
Project D has the higher accounting rate of return and is therefore preferred by this method.

QUESTIONS

3.1 What is the basis of the payback method of investment appraisal?
3.2 Discuss the main shortcomings of the payback approach. Illustrate your answer by reference to the first worked example above.
3.3 To what extent do you agree with the view that payback provides an in-built safeguard against risk?
3.4 What are the advantages which the accounting rate of return approach has over payback?
3.5 Are these advantages sufficient to make its use desirable? Why or why not?
3.6 Using the second of the worked examples above to illustrate your arguments, discuss the shortcomings of the accounting rate of return approach.

4 DISCOUNTING TECHNIQUES OF INVESTMENT APPRAISAL

Introduction

This chapter sets out the two main discounting techniques of investment appraisal: namely the net present value (NPV) method and the internal rate of return (IRR) method. In order to gain an understanding of these techniques we will continue with the simplifying assumption adopted in Chapter 2 and also used in Chapter 3 that the sums of money resulting from an investment which accrue in the future are known with certainty. In addition, the assumption that there is no inflation will continue to be made. In later chapters these assumptions will be dropped and techniques for dealing with these real-world complexities will be considered.

We have already stressed that if investment decisions are to be made which are consistent with the goals of the organization, it is necessary to take account of the time value of money. Both the NPV and the IRR methods have the advantage that they discount future sums of money to be received or to be expended. For this reason both techniques are considered to be 'scientific' methods of investment appraisal. However, two caveats are necessary when making this claim. First, while the techniques do provide definite decision advice when cash flows are known with certainty and there is zero inflation, in practice such conditions do not hold and it is therefore necessary to augment the use of the techniques with judgement and experience. In other words, the 'scientific' label does not mean that the techniques should be used as hard-and-fast decision rules. The techniques exist to assist the decision-making process, they do not exist to replace the decision-making process. Second, while both techniques are considered 'scientific', under particular circumstances they will give different rankings of investment opportunities. Clearly, only one ranking can be considered correct and it is important to know which it is. For this reason, the explanation of the techniques will be followed by a discussion of the relative attributes of the two techniques so that we can achieve an understanding of which technique is most appropriate.

In the discussion of the techniques which follows, the concepts of the time value of money, discounting and present values which were set out in Chapter 2 will be used extensively. The arguments presented in that chapter will not be repeated here.

The NPV method of investment appraisal was implicitly considered in Chapter 2 in considering the investment for which cash flows were shown in Table 2.2 and comparing the present value of those cash flows with the sum required for the investment. Explicitly, the NPV method involves comparing the *present value* of the future cash flows of an investment opportunity with the cash outlay which is required to finance the opportunity. In this way we can determine whether the investment opportunity provides a *surplus* when the cash flows are measured in present-value terms. The stages involved in using the NPV method are as follows:

I.   estimate all future net cash flows (revenues minus costs) associated with an investment opportunity;
II.   convert these net cash flow figures to their present-value equivalents by discounting at the appropriate discount rate (the choice of the discount rate will be discussed in Chapter 9);
III. sum all of the present-value figures for future cash flows;
IV.   subtract from this value the initial cost of the investment.

The resulting figure from these calculations is the net present value. Mathematically, the NPV is calculated by using the following formula:

$$NPV = \frac{A_1}{(1 + r)} + \frac{A_2}{(1 + r)^2} + \frac{A_3}{(1 + r)^3} + \ldots + \frac{A_n}{(1 + r)^n} - I_0 = \sum_{t=1}^{t=n} \frac{A_t}{(1 + r)^t} - I_0,$$

where A_t is the net cash flow in year t, n is the number of years for which the project will generate cash flows, I_0 is the initial investment required, r is the appropriate discount rate.

The figure calculated from this formula measures the surplus which is made as a result of undertaking the project in excess of that which could be made by investing at the marginal rate of return. If the NPV is positive, the investment generates a surplus and the investment will increase the wealth of the shareholders. If the NPV is negative the 'surplus' is actually a deficit and undertaking the investment would reduce the wealth of the shareholders. Thus, under conditions of certainty the NPV method provides definite decision advice for independent investment projects: undertake those investment opportunities for which there is a positive NPV and do not undertake those investments for which the NPV is negative. Similarly, when projects are mutually exclusive, NPV provides definite ranking advice: undertake the investment opportunity which has the highest NPV, providing that the NPV of this investment is positive. If it is negative, do not undertake any of the investment opportunities.

The use of NPV can be illustrated using an example. Consider a firm which is considering introducing a new line of men's jackets. Production of the new jacket will require new factory space and equipment. The firm can either construct a purpose-built factory on a site it has identified or it can refit a factory which it owns and which is currently lying idle. While the purpose-built factory involves a higher initial cost, the running of the new factory will be

Table 4.1 Project A

Year n	Cash inflow (£000)	Discount by $(1 + r)^n$	Present value (£000)
0	−2,000	1	−2,000
1	350	1.1	318.18
2	500	1.21	413.22
3	600	1.331	450.79
4	800	1.4641	546.41
5	800	1.6105	496.74
6	600	1.7716	338.68

Table 4.2 Project B

Year n	Cash inflow (£000)	Discount by $(1+r)^n$	Present value (£000)
0	−1,500	1	−1,500
1	200	1.1	181.82
2	260	1.21	214.88
3	450	1.331	338.09
4	700	1.4641	478.11
5	700	1.6105	434.64
6	400	1.7716	225.79

cheaper due to its being of an overall more appropriate design for the purpose for which it will be used than is the refit factory. The firm is thus faced with choice of mutually exclusive investment opportunities. The net cash flow associated with the purpose-built factory (project A) and the refit factory (project B) are shown in Tables 4.1 and 4.2, as are the present values of these cash flows for a discount rate of 10%.

The NPV for project A is £564,020 and that for project B is £373,330. Thus while project A has a higher initial cost, the higher running costs of project mean that the surplus created by project A is greater. Given that the project with the higher NPV has a positive NPV, the firm should go ahead with project A. The surplus of the project means that shareholder wealth will be increased by undertaking this investment opportunity, and will be increased by more than if project B were undertaken.

Clearly, if projects A and B were independent projects, rather than mutually exclusive investment opportunities, then the firm would maximize the increase in shareholder wealth by undertaking both projects.

THE INTERNAL RATE OF RETURN (IRR) METHOD OF INVESTMENT APPRAISAL

The IRR method of investment appraisal has strong similarities to the NPV method, but, as stated above, despite these similarities the IRR method can produce different rankings of investment opportunities. A variation on the NPV equation given above provides the basis for calculating the IRR. The IRR is the value of the discount rate in the NPV equation which leads to a value for the NPV of zero.

Thus, the IRR is found by solving for IRR in the following equation:

$$0 = \frac{A_1}{(1 + IRR)} + \frac{A_2}{(1 + IRR)^2} + \frac{A_3}{(1 + IRR)^3} + \ldots + \frac{A_n}{(1 + IRR)^n} - I_0 = \sum_{t=1}^{t=n} \frac{A_t}{(1 + IRR)^t} - I_0$$

The value of IRR calculated from this formula provides a measure of the rate of return earned on that capital which is used in the project during the time that the capital is used, after allowing for the recoupment of the initial capital outlay. Having determined the IRR by using the above formula, we can reach a decision on whether to go ahead with the project by comparing the IRR with the firm's cost of capital (its discount rate). For independent investment opportunities, if the IRR is greater than the cost of capital then the project should be undertaken, since a rate of return is being earned by the project which is greater than the amount which has to be paid out to the providers of capital. Thus the project is earning a surplus over and above the cost of funds and thus shareholder wealth will be increased. If the IRR is less than the cost of capital then the project should not be undertaken as going ahead with the project will have the result of reducing shareholder wealth. For mutually exclusive investment opportunities the IRR decision rule involves undertaking that investment which has the highest IRR, provided that the IRR is greater than the cost of capital. While the IRR is described as an investment appraisal technique, it would be more accurate to describe it as an arithmetic artefact since it is simply the solution value for a discount rate for an equation. In practice the IRR method provides no new information over and above that provided by the NPV method of investment appraisal. However, according to a number of studies IRR is more widely used than is NPV. For example, Sangster (1993) finds that of the firms in his sample 58% used IRR whereas only 48% used NPV. The main reason for this appears to be that people in business are more used to thinking in terms of rates of return than in terms of NPVs or 'surpluses'.

The use of IRR is illustrated by using the same example as was used for the NPV method above, as shown in Tables 4.1 and 4.2. The firm's cost of capital is still assumed to be 10% (the discount rate used in Tables 4.1 and 4.2). Finding the IRR of a project is essentially a matter of trial and error, although in practice many computer packages and calculators can be used to find the IRR. For the projects shown in Tables 4.1 and 4.2, the NPV was positive when a discount rate of 10% was used. It therefore follows that the IRR must be greater than 10%. Tables 4.3 and 4.4 show the present value figures when a discount rate of 15% is used.

With a discount rate of 15% the NPV of project A is £191,440, while that of project B is £87,570. Thus the IRR for both projects must be above 15%. Repeating this exercise with a discount rate of 20% yields NPV figures of (−£105,646) for project A and (−£139,511) for project B. Hence, by trial and error it has been established that the IRR for both projects must lie between 15%

Table 4.3 Project A

Year n	Cash inflow (£000)	Discount by $(1 + r)^n$	Present value (£000)
0	−2,000	1	−2,000
1	350	1.15	304.35
2	500	1.3225	378.07
3	600	1.5209	394.50
4	800	1.7490	457.40
5	800	2.0114	397.73
6	600	2.3131	259.39

Table 4.4 Project B

Year n	Cash inflow (£000)	Discount by $(1 + r)^n$	Present value (£000)
0	−1,500	1	−1,500
1	200	1.15	173.91
2	260	1.3225	196.60
3	450	1.5209	295.88
4	700	1.7490	400.23
5	700	2.0114	348.02
6	400	2.3131	172.93

and 20%. By continuing with this trial-and-error process it can be established that the IRR for project A is 18.1%, while that for project B is 16.8%. Since project A has the higher IRR and since the IRR for this project is greater than the firm's cost of capital of 10%, the IRR decision rule suggests that the firm should go ahead with project A. This is in line with the decision advice of the NPV method.

While the trial-and-error method shown provides a very accurate means of establishing the IRR of the projects, it is clearly very time-consuming in the absence of a programmable calculator or a computer package which calculates the IRR for you. An alternative method involves using the technique of interpolation. While this does not provide a value for the IRR which is exactly correct, it does give a close approximation. To use the technique of interpolation it is first necessary to determine a discount rate which generates a (preferably small) negative NPV and another discount rate which generates a (preferably small) positive NPV. The accuracy of the technique is determined by how close the two NPV figures are to zero. If the figures are a long way from zero, the estimate of the IRR will be less accurate for reasons set out below. Having established these discount values for a negative and a positive NPV figure it must be the case that the IRR falls somewhere between the two. Interpolation can then be used to determine the discount rate which yields a zero NPV figure by assuming that the relationship between NPV and the discount rate is linear, i.e. that a one-point decrease in the discount rate always generates the same increase in the NPV. The fact that the relationship between NPV and the discount rate is not linear is the reason why this technique only provides an approximate value for the IRR and why it is first of all necessary to find NPV figures (one above and one below zero) which are close to zero. The actual relationship between the NPV and the discount rate is shown in Figure 4.1. The dashed line represents a linear relationship and demonstrates that such a relationship is only an approximation to the true curve. The further away the figures are from zero the less accurate is the assumption of a linear relationship.

In the above example it has been shown that with a discount rate of 15% the NPV for A is £191,440 while that for project B is £87,570. Similarly the NPVs for the two projects when the discount rate is 20% are (−£105,646) and (−£139,511) respectively. Thus for project A, increasing the discount rate by 5% leads to a fall in the NPV of £297,086 (£191,440 + £105,646). By assuming a linear relationship, this figure can then be used as a basis for determining how big the increase in the discount rate from 15% should be to lead to a reduction of £191,440 (i.e. to obtain a figure for the NPV of zero):

$$\frac{191{,}440}{297{,}086} \times 5\% = 0.644 \times 5\% = 3.2\%.$$

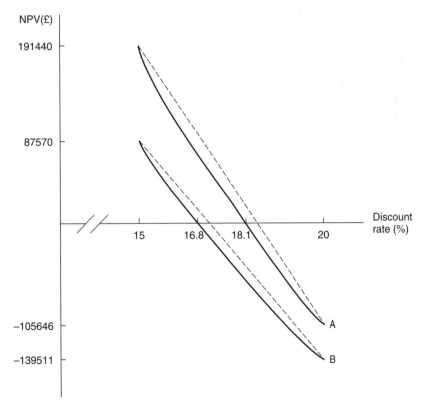

Figure 4.1
Estimation of the IRR by linear interpolation

Thus the IRR for project A can be seen to be approximately 18.2%. This compares with the figure shown above (the accurate figure) of 18.1%. Following the same procedure for project B we can determine an approximate value for its IRR:

$$\frac{87,570}{227,081} \times 5\% = 0.386 \times 5\% = 1.9\%.$$

Thus for project B the IRR is approximately 16.9% when calculated by interpolation, compared to the actual figure of 16.8%.

We have stressed above that the accuracy of interpolation depends upon the closeness to zero of the two NPV figures used. This is borne out by the fact that if the NPV figures from using discount rates of 10% and 20% were used as the basis for interpolation, the results would be less accurate at 18.4% for project A and 17.2% for project B. While it does not alter the ranking of projects in this case, it is possible that if figures a long way from zero are used as the basis for interpolation then the rankings could be reversed. Thus it is important to get NPV figures above and below zero which are close to zero before using the process of interpolation.

In the examples of projects A and B used above, the NPV method and the IRR method resulted in the same ranking of projects. However, there are some situations in which the two methods will generate different rankings of projects. It is therefore important to understand fully the relative merits of NPV and IRR and why the two methods can generate different rankings. To achieve this we need to make a comparison of the two approaches to investment appraisal.

NPV AND IRR COMPARED

In all of the discussion which has taken place in this book up to this point we have stressed the need to take account of the time value of money and to discount future sums to their present value. Failure to do this will lead to decisions being taken which may be at variance with the goals of the owners of the organization on whose behalf the decisions are being made. As we have seen in this chapter, both the NPV and the IRR methods have the advantage that they take account of the time value of money and thus they are viewed as superior to the non-discounting techniques set out in the previous chapter. In addition, these two techniques have the advantage that they focus on cash flows rather than on accounting profits.

Given that both NPV and IRR are characterized by these advantages it may be thought that either is equally acceptable in terms of providing decision advice which helps to meet the goals of the organization. However, while the two techniques are clearly similar, they do not always guarantee to provide the same investment decision advice. We therefore need to make a comparison of the two techniques to understand which is superior. This is particularly important because, as we will see, while IRR tends to be more popular with business decision makers, it is the NPV approach which is more reliable. The preference of decision makers for IRR results from the fact that business people are more used to thinking in terms of rates of return. However, in some situations the use of the IRR approach may lead to inappropriate investment decision guidance. It is helpful to undertake the comparison of the two techniques under six different scenarios. Before doing this, however, it is helpful to define two terms: orthodox cash flows and unorthodox cash flows.

An orthodox cash flow is one where an initial cash outflow is followed by a series of net cash inflows, with no periods involving a further net cash outflow. Projects A and B discussed above involve cash flows with such a pattern and therefore would be described as projects with orthodox cash flows. With an orthodox cash flow there is only one 'change of sign', i.e. one time where there is a shift from either a negative or a positive cash flow to a cash flow of the opposite sign. With projects A and B the change of sign occurs in year 1 and there is no further change of sign. Thus the cash flow pattern is of the form: −, +, +, +, +, +, +.

In contrast, an unorthodox cash flow involves more than one change of sign. For example, consider the cash flows for project C, shown in Table 4.5. These are identical to the cash flows for project A (Table 4.1 above), except that in year 7 there is a further net cash outflow (this could arise from, say, needing to demolish the factory and landscape the countryside).

The cash flows for project C are 'unorthodox' as there is more than one change of sign. In this example there are two changes of sign: from negative to positive in year 1 and from positive to negative in year 7; and the cash flows are of the form: −, +, +, +, +, +, +, −. It is quite possible that for some projects there will be more changes of sign than there are for project C. For example, if a large refurbishment is required at some point in a project's life, there may be a period of net cash inflows, then a net cash outflow, which is then followed by further net cash inflows. Thus, for example, the cash flows could take the form: −, +, +, +, −, +, +, +. In this case there are three changes of sign: in year 1 (negative to positive), in year 4 (positive to negative) and in year 5 (negative to positive). The distinction between orthodox and unorthodox cash flows becomes important in considering the relative merits of the NPV and IRR approaches to investment appraisal.

Table 4.5 Project C

Year n	Cash inflow (£000)	Discount by $(1 + r)^n$	Present value (£000)
0	−2,000	1	−2,000
1	350	1.1	318.18
2	500	1.21	413.22
3	600	1.331	450.79
4	800	1.4641	546.41
5	800	1.6105	496.74
6	600	1.7716	338.68
7	−200	1.9487	−102.63

Independent projects with no capital rationing

In situations where projects are independent and there is no restriction on the level of investment to be undertaken, a firm would undertake all projects that are consistent with its goals. This involves choosing to go ahead with all projects for which the NPV is positive or for which the IRR is greater than the firm's cost of capital. All such projects will lead to an increase in shareholder wealth and can be considered to be 'profitable' (using this term loosely, rather than in an accounting sense), given the firm's cost of capital.

In such a situation the advice given by both NPV and IRR about which investment opportunities to undertake and which to reject will be identical provided that the cash flows of the projects are orthodox. Under these circumstances both techniques give unequivocal (under the continued assumption of certainty) and acceptable investment-decision advice. For this reason either technique can be used without concern about conflicting advice. However, a problem arises from the fact that such a situation rarely, if ever, occurs, since in practice projects are frequently not independent and capital may well be rationed (this issue is discussed more fully in Chapter 8). We therefore need to consider more realistic situations and compare the two techniques under these circumstances.

Projects with unorthodox cash flows

In discussing the IRR rule above, this technique for investment appraisal was described as an arithmetic artefact. The fact that the IRR is simply the solution to an equation raises a potentially important problem when this approach is adopted for appraising investment opportunities which are characterized by unorthodox cash flows. The reason for this can best be understood by considering a project which requires an initial investment immediately and which generates cash flows in two subsequent periods (making three periods in total). In such a situation the IRR is found by solving the following equation:

$$0 = \sum_{t=1}^{t=2} \frac{A_t}{(1 + IRR)^t} - I_0 = \frac{A_1}{(1 + IRR)} + \frac{A_2}{(1 + IRR)^2} - I_0.$$

Multiplying both sides of this equation by $(1+IRR)^2$ gives:

$$0 = -I_0 (1 + IRR)^2 + A_1 (1 + IRR) + A_2.$$

The above equation is a quadratic equation and standard mathematics states that as such it will have two roots (two values of IRR) which make the two sides equal. If there were three cash flows after the initial investment then we would have a four-period example, the equation would be of a cubic form and there would be three roots which solve the equation. More generally, this type of formula is known as a polynomial of degree n (where n is the total number of periods) and there will be $n - 1$ values of IRR which solve the equation.

The existence of more than one solution value for IRR clearly poses a potential problem for the decision maker. For example, if there are two values of IRR of 10% and 20%, and the cost of capital is 15% then there is ambiguous advice from the IRR rule. Such a situation is illustrated in Figure 4.2.

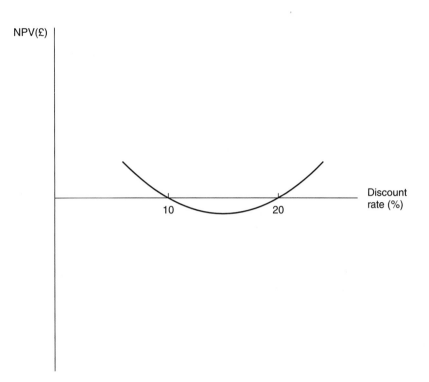

NPV(£)

10   20   Discount rate (%)

Figure 4.2
Unorthodox cash flows and
two values of IRR

With more than one value of IRR it is not easy to determine which is the value that should be used. In contrast, the NPV approach will generate only one figure. In practice, the multiple roots problem is not as great as appears at first sight (although the roots problem is always severe for hairdressers!). The reason for this is that many of the values of IRR which solve the equation can be ignored because they are negative or imaginary. For example, if values of IRR which solve the equation are 15% and −15%, only the first of these is economically (as opposed to mathematically) meaningful. In the case of orthodox cash flows there will indeed be only one positive (i.e. economically meaningful) value of IRR which solves the equation. (This follows from Descartes's change-of-sign rule which shows that there will be one positive solution (root) for each change of sign (change in cash flow from negative to positive or positive to negative). As was seen above, orthodox cash flows have only one change of sign.) Thus for orthodox cash flows the multiple roots problem does not exist.

However, when there is an unorthodox cash flow there may be more than one positive root (one positive value of IRR) which solves the equation and it is then difficult to decide which should be used as the basis for decision making, as was seen in Figure 4.2. Indeed, more complicated situations can arise, as shown in Figure 4.3. In this situation there are three values of IRR: 7%, 12% and 20%. With a cost of capital of, say, 16%, it may be thought that the investment opportunity should be rejected on the grounds that two of the IRRs are below the cost of capital. However, as is shown in Figure 4.3, the investment opportunity yields a positive NPV when a discount rate of 16% is used.

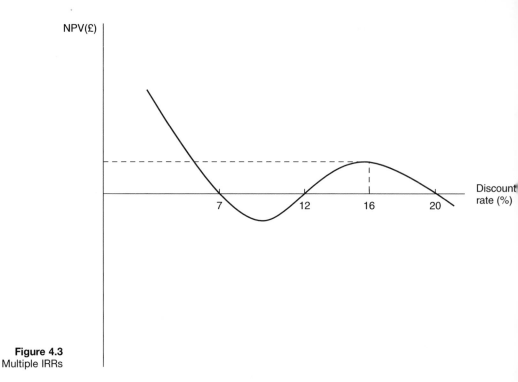

Figure 4.3
Multiple IRRs

In the case of unorthodox cash flows another problem can emerge, even when there are not multiple roots. Such a situation is illustrated in Figure 4.4. In this case there is only one positive value of IRR (15%), but the investment opportunity never yields a positive NPV. If the cost of capital for the firm considering this project is 10%, the IRR rule would incorrectly suggest acceptance of the project. The diagram shows that at a discount rate of 10% the NPV is negative.

In practice many of the problems of multiple roots do not materialize. Either there is only one positive economically meaningful value of IRR, or in the case of multiple roots all of the values fall either below or above the cost of capital and the decision advice is unambiguous. Nonetheless, in the case of unorthodox cash flows there are potential problems with IRR which do not exist with the NPV approach. Further problems with the IRR approach are identified when we move away from the situation of independent projects with no capital rationing.

Mutually exclusive investment opportunities with the same capital outlay

In many practical situations firms are faced with mutually exclusive investment opportunities where acceptance of one opportunity necessarily means that another will not be undertaken. For example, a company may be considering purchasing a new computer system for its offices. There may be two competing

Discounting Techniques of Investment Appraisal

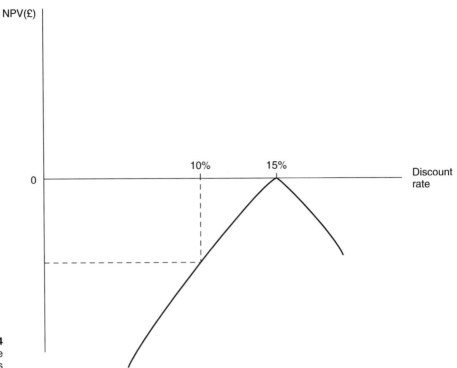

Figure 4.4
Negative NPVs and positive
IRRs

systems which will both do the tasks required and the company must make an
'either/or' choice. In such a situation it has been seen that the NPV rule states
that the project with the higher NPV should be accepted (assuming the NPV is
positive), while the IRR rule states that the project with the higher IRR should
be accepted (again assuming that the IRR is greater than the cost of capital).
Unfortunately, there are circumstances in which the advice given by the NPV
rule will conflict with that given by the IRR rule. Such a situation exists in the
example for the cash flows for projects D and E shown in Table 4.6, using a
discount rate of 10%.

In this example, the NPV rule suggests that project D should be accepted,
while the IRR rule suggests project E should be accepted. Clearly, both rules
cannot be giving the correct advice. In fact it is the NPV rule which gives the
'correct' advice, while the IRR is 'at fault'. The conflict in advice can be understood by considering Figure 4.5. This plots the NPV of the two projects for
discount rates from 0% to 25%. As can be seen from the diagram, the NPV of
project D is greater than that of project E for discount rates up to approximately
12.67%. For discount rates above this figure, the NPV of project D is less than
the NPV of project E. The figure of 12.67% is the discount rate at which the two
projects have the same NPV. This is the point where the NPV curves intersect.

For the NPV and IRR methods to give conflicting advice in this type of
situation the NPV curves must intersect, the point of intersection must be at
a discount rate to the right of (i.e. greater than) the cost of capital (the NPV

Table 4.6 Projects D and E

Year n	Project D cash inflow (£000)	Project E cash inflow (£000)
0	−2,000	−2,000
1	0	500
2	0	500
3	0	500
4	100	500
5	200	500
6	2,000	500
7	2,500	500
NPV	604.3	434.2
IRR	14.6%	16.3%

discount rate) and the point of intersection must be in the positive (north-east) quadrant. The IRR rule can be shown to be 'at fault' in these circumstances by considering the hypothetical incremental cash flows of the two projects. To do this we subtract the cash flows associated with project E from those associated with project D to create the cash flows for the hypothetical project D − E as shown in Table 4.7.

The IRR for the 'project D − E' can be calculated as 12.67%. We can use this result to demonstrate that the IRR rule generated inaccurate advice in the first place. On the basis of the IRR rule project E should be accepted. We can now consider whether it is also worthwhile investing in the hypothetical

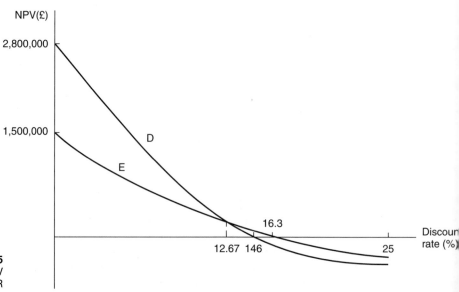

Figure 4.5
Conflicting advice from NPV
and IRR

Discounting Techniques of Investment Appraisal

Table 4.7 Projects D, E and D − E

Year n	Project D cash inflow (£000)	Project E cash inflow (£000)	'Project D − E' cash inflow (£000)
0	−2,000	−2,000	0
1	0	500	−500
2	0	500	−500
3	0	500	−500
4	100	500	−400
5	200	500	−300
6	2,000	500	1,500
7	2,500	500	2,000

project D − E. The IRR for D − E is 12.67%, which is above the cost of capital of 10%. Therefore project D − E is also worth undertaking. On the basis of the IRR rule the investment advice is to undertake project E and undertake project D − E. Since E + D − E = D, only project D should be undertaken and the IRR rule has been used to demonstrate that the IRR rule gave inaccurate advice in the first place.

The IRR rule has been used to demonstrate that the NPV rule gave the correct advice initially. The reason for the conflict in advice in this example is that the two techniques of investment appraisal make different assumptions regarding what will happen to cash inflows from investment projects.

When cash flows are received from a project the firm which has made the investment will have that money available to use as it so chooses. The money can either be reinvested (thus avoiding raising new funds from providers of capital) or it can be used to repay funds to the providers of capital. Thus when cash flows are received the company can be thought of as making a saving in terms of payments to the providers of funds. This saving is sometimes referred to as the 'reinvestment rate of interest', but more properly should be referred to as the 'opportunity cost of funds' (the rate that would have to be paid to the providers of funds if funds were not available from the project's cash flows). The NPV method of investment appraisal makes no assumptions about reinvestment of cash flows, but it is implicit in this approach that any interim cash flows from a project will be reinvested or will have an opportunity cost equal to the project discount rate. This clearly makes sense, since the discount rate reflects the cost of funds. However, implicit in the IRR method is the notion that cash flows from a project will be reinvested or will have an opportunity cost of capital equal to the IRR of the project which is generating the cash flows. Such an assumption (albeit an implicit assumption) is unwarranted, since the rate of return on a particular project relates to that project only. Simply because a firm faces one investment opportunity paying a rate of return of, say, 25%, does not mean that it faces other investment opportunities paying that rate of return. Thus, the IRR is making an inappropriate assumption about the use of interim cash flows and will therefore implicitly favour projects which earn higher cash flows earlier to an extent which is unwarranted by the time value of money. The assumption implicit in the NPV approach is completely consistent with the opportunity cost of funds and as such provides correct decision advice, whereas the IRR approach is not always reliable.

Mutually exclusive investment opportunities with different levels of capital outlay

The example discussed above related to differences in ranking for two projects with the same level of initial investment. Another problem regarding ranking of projects emerges when considering mutually exclusive investment opportunities which require different levels of initial investment. Consider, for example the projects E (the same as above) and F (an alternative to E with a lower capital outlay) shown in Table 4.8 for a discount rate of 10%.

Once again there is a difference in ranking between the two methods of investment appraisal, with the NPV method ranking project E more highly and the IRR method giving project F the higher ranking. As was the case previously the NPV method gives reliable decision advice, while the IRR method provides investment advice which is unreliable. The basic problem in this case is that the IRR approach 'prefers' a project which offers a higher rate of return, irrespective of the scale of the investment. In this example, 25.5% rate of return on £500,000 is 'preferred' by the IRR method to 16.3% return on £2,000,000. In undertaking investment appraisal it is important to compare 'like with like'. If project E yields 16.3% return on £2,000,000, the question the decision maker should be asking is 'What return will I get on £2,000,000 if I invest some of it (£500,000) in project F and the rest in another project?' Again, it is necessary to consider the opportunity cost of capital. If only £500,000 is required for this investment then savings will be made compared to undertaking project E in

Table 4.8 Projects E and F

Year n	Project E cash inflow (£000)	Project F cash inflow (£000)
0	−2,000	−500
1	500	160
2	500	160
3	500	160
4	500	160
5	500	160
6	500	160
7	500	160
NPV	434.2	278.9
IRR	16.3%	25.5%

Discounting Techniques of Investment Appraisal

terms of payments to providers of capital, since the extra £1,500,000 does not have to be raised. The rate of return saved will be the opportunity cost of capital, which is equal to the discount rate. Thus, while project F yields 25.5% return, the total return (return on project F plus savings on payments to providers of capital) on £2,000,000 is:

$$\frac{500,000}{2,000,000} \times 25.5\% + \frac{1,500,000}{2,000,000} \times 10\% = 13.875\%.$$

Thus it is clear that the return on £2,000,000 is greater when project E is undertaken than when project F is undertaken together with a saving in payments to providers of capital. The NPV approach correctly identifies project E as the desirable project because it implicitly takes account of the scale of the initial investment.

Mutually exclusive investment opportunities with different lengths of lives

A further problem with the IRR approach can be identified when we consider mutually exclusive investment opportunities which have different lengths of life. Consider, for example, projects G and H as shown in Table 4.9. The discount rate is assumed to be 10%.

The examples in Table 4.9 again illustrate a potential for differences in ranking. While the scales of the investment in terms of initial outlay are the same for the two projects, the life of project H is longer than that of project G. Thus while project G offers a 25% rate of return on the initial investment, the return is only earned for one year. In contrast, while project H offers a lower rate of return, this return is earned over a longer (three-year) period. While project G generates cash flows earlier, the funds generated have an opportunity cost of 10% (the discount rate) for the same reason as stated in the discussion above. As the NPV approach automatically takes account of the length of life of investment opportunities, once again this approach provides reliable investment decision advice.

Table 4.9 Projects G and H

Year n	Project G cash inflow (£000)	Project H cash inflow (£000)
0	−3,000	−3,000
1	3,750	0
2	0	0
3	0	5,000
NPV	409.1	756.6
IRR	25%	18.6%

Investment opportunities with capital rationing

In situations where funds for investment are rationed it will not be possible to undertake all investment opportunities which have a positive NPV or for which the IRR is greater than the cost of capital, even where the projects are not mutually exclusive. Capital rationing raises problems for both the NPV method and the IRR method and so we will have a chapter devoted to this topic alone. The problems posed by capital rationing will therefore not be discussed here, but will be addressed in Chapter 8. However, at this stage it is worth pointing out that the NPV method should still be used as the basis for investment decisions even in these circumstances, although some modification to the decision-making criteria needs to be made.

SUMMARY AND KEY POINTS

This chapter has set out the two so-called 'scientific' approaches to investment appraisal. It has been shown that both techniques are superior to the non-discounting approaches discussed in the previous chapter because both the NPV and the IRR have the advantage that they take account of the time value of money and discount future sums of money to be received and expended. However, it has also been stressed that in some circumstances the IRR approach is unreliable, whereas the NPV approach always provides decision advice which is consistent with the goals of the organization, unless capital is rationed. This problem will be discussed in detail in Chapter 8. In addition, despite this strong claim in favour of the NPV approach, we need to remember that investment appraisal techniques do not provide hard-and-fast decision rules. Rather they should be used to guide and inform the decision-making process. The key points from this chapter are as follows:

- If investment decisions are to be made which are consistent with the goals of the organization, it is necessary to take account of the time value of money.
- The NPV method involves comparing the *present value* of the future cash flows of an investment opportunity with the cash outlay which is required to finance the opportunity.
- The NPV measures the surplus which is made as a result of undertaking the project in excess of that which could be made by investing at the marginal rate of return.
- Under conditions of certainty the NPV method provides definite decision advice for independent investment projects: undertake those investment opportunities for which there is a positive NPV and do not undertake those investments for which the NPV is negative.
- When projects are mutually exclusive, NPV also provides definite ranking advice: undertake the investment opportunity which has the highest NPV, providing that the NPV of this investment is positive.
- The IRR is the value of the discount rate in the NPV equation which leads to a value for the NPV of zero.

- The IRR provides a measure of the rate of return earned on that capital which is used in the project during the time that the capital is used, after allowing for the recoupment of the initial capital outlay.
- For independent investment opportunities if the IRR is greater than the cost of capital then the project should be undertaken.
- For mutually exclusive investment opportunities the IRR decision rule involves undertaking that investment which has the highest IRR, provided that the IRR is greater than the cost of capital.
- In practice the IRR method provides no new information over and above that provided by the NPV method of investment appraisal and is simply an arithmetic artefact.
- While the NPV and IRR techniques do provide definite decision advice when cash flows are known with certainty and there is zero inflation, in practice such conditions do not hold and it is therefore necessary to augment the use of the techniques with judgement and experience.
- While IRR tends to be more popular with business decision makers, it is the NPV approach which is more reliable since in some situations the use of the IRR approach may lead to inappropriate investment-decision guidance.
- In situations where projects are independent and there is no restriction on the level of investment to be undertaken the advice given by both NPV and IRR about which investment opportunities to undertake and which to reject will be identical provided that the cash flows of the projects are orthodox.
- In the case of unorthodox cash flows there are potential problems with IRR which do not exist with the NPV approach.
- With mutually exclusive investments the NPV method gives reliable decision advice, while the IRR method may provide investment advice which is unreliable.
- Capital rationing raises problems for both the NPV method and the IRR method (see Chapter 8).

WORKED EXAMPLE

A company has a factory site which is currently unused and is considering two, mutually exclusive, uses of the site. The estimated net cash flows from the two potential projects are as shown in the table.

Year	Cash flow – project A (£s)	Cash flow – project B (£s)
0	−150,000	−150,000
1	50,000	120,000
2	50,000	25,000
3	50,000	25,000
4	50,000	25,000
5	50,000	25,000

You are required to:

(a) Calculate the NPV of the two projects when the discount rate is 10%.
(b) Calculate the IRR of the two projects.
(c) Decide which project is 'preferred' by NPV and which by IRR.
(d) Explain why there is a difference in ranking between the NPV and IRR methods.
(e) Decide which method of investment appraisal provides the correct answer.

Illustrate your answer by reference to the hypothetical cash flow A − B.

Answers:

(a)

Year n	Cash inflow Project A (£)	Cash inflow Project B (£)	Discount by $(1 + r)^n$	Present value Project A (£)	Present value Project B (£)
0	−150,000	−150,000	1	−150,000	−150,000
1	50,000	120,000	1.1	45,455	109,091
2	50,000	25,000	1.21	41,322	20,661
3	50,000	25,000	1.331	37,566	18,783
4	50,000	25,000	1.4641	34,151	17,075
5	50,000	25,000	1.6105	31,046	15,523

NPV_A = 45,455 + 41,322 + 37,566 + 34,151 + 31,046 − 150,000 = £39,540
NPV_B = 109,091 + 20,661 + 18,783 + 17,075 + 15,523 − 150,000 = £31,133

(b) Given that both projects have a positive NPV when the discount rate is 10%, the IRR must be greater than 10% for each project. Repeating the above analysis using a discount rate of 20%, we find that the NPV of A is −£469 and the NPV of B is £3,932. With a discount rate of 22% the NPV of B is −£540. Therefore, the IRR of A is just below 20%, while that of B is just below 22%. (Using a spreadsheet package or a programmable calculator we can find that IRR_A is 19.86%, while IRR_B is 21.75%.)

(c) If we use the NPV method, then project A would be chosen. If we use the IRR method, then project B would be chosen.

(d) The difference in ranking arises because of the different implicit assumptions about reinvestment rates. IRR implicitly assumes that a project's cash flows can be reinvested at the IRR, which is incorrect. As a result of this implicit assumption, it prefers projects such as B which have large cash flows in the earlier years.

(e) The NPV method provides the correct answer. We can illustrate this by considering the cash flows of the hypothetical project (A − B):

Year n	Project A cash inflow (£)	Project B cash inflow (£)	'Project A − B' cash inflow (£)
0	−150,000	−150,000	0
1	50,000	120,000	−70,000
2	50,000	25,000	25,000
3	50,000	25,000	25,000
4	50,000	25,000	25,000
5	50,000	25,000	25,000

Using a discount rate of 10%, we find that the NPV of the hypothetical project is £8,406. Similarly, with a discount rate of 15% it is £1,195 and using a discount rate of 16% it is (−£39). Therefore the IRR of the hypothetical project is just below 16% (actually, it is 15.97%). As this is higher than the discount rate of 10%, IRR says to accept the hypothetical project A − B, as well as accepting project B. Thus, IRR says accept B + A − B = A. Using the IRR method, it has been shown that the IRR method gave incorrect advice in the first place.

QUESTIONS

4.1 Explain what the NPV of a project represents and state why the use of the NPV method enables decisions to be taken which are consistent with the goals of a private-sector organization.

4.2 What does the IRR represent?

4.3 In what circumstances are the NPV and IRR methods guaranteed to give the same investment-decision advice?

4.4 What is an unorthodox cash flow and why does it cause problems for investment appraisal?

4.5 Why might the NPV and IRR methods give different rankings for mutually exclusive investment opportunities?

5 INVESTMENT DECISION MAKING UNDER CONDITIONS OF UNCERTAINTY: PROBLEMS AND SIMPLE SOLUTIONS

Introduction

We have seen that the investment decision criterion is straightforward under conditions of certainty and no capital rationing: for independent projects investors should undertake all investments which offer a positive net present value (NPV), while for mutually exclusive projects that which has the highest NPV should be undertaken provided that the NPV is positive. However, in discussing investment appraisal techniques and in establishing the superiority of the NPV approach, we have stressed that the NPV method should not be used as a hard-and-fast decision rule. Rather, the use of the method should be augmented with the use of judgement and experience. The reason for this is quite simple: in practice, for the vast majority of investments the cash flows associated with the investment project are not known with certainty at the time the investment decision is taken. While discounting future cash flows is an appropriate means for taking account of the time value of money, it does not deal with the problem of uncertainty over future cash flows. The problem of uncertainty is pervasive in investment appraisal and decision makers need to be aware of the difficulties which uncertainty can cause and of the means which are available for assisting the decision-making process in the presence of uncertainty. It is these issues which we address in this chapter and the next.

In discussing the problems caused by the absence of certainty and the methods available for assisting decision makers under such conditions, the superiority of the NPV approach, established in Chapter 4, will be assumed. Thus, in discussing techniques available to the decision maker under conditions of uncertainty, we take as the starting point the NPV method, and developments of this method will be utilized. In addition, the problems caused by capital rationing will not be considered here, but will be discussed in detail in Chapter 8. In this chapter we give consideration to what might be described as simple *ad hoc* methods for dealing with uncertainty, rather than to more complicated methods or methods based on any formal theory.

In this way, simple, practical, intuitive means for addressing difficulties associated with the absence of certainty regarding future cash flows will be considered. In the next chapter we consider more advanced methods, but again these will not be based on formal theory. However, as we will see, the use of the techniques discussed in this chapter and in Chapter 6 introduces some subjectivity into the decision-making process and it is, therefore, desirable to also have a more formal, objective approach to dealing with these problems. Such an approach is considered in Chapter 7. Before going on to discuss the various techniques which are available to assist the decision maker who is faced with uncertainty, it is helpful to consider the nature and sources of uncertainty and the different attitudes which individuals can take to a lack of certainty.

DISTINGUISHING BETWEEN RISK AND UNCERTAINTY

In the discussion so far, we have made reference to conditions where cash flows are known with certainty and to cash flows which are uncertain. The latter term has been taken to mean conditions where such certainty does not hold. The existence or otherwise of certainty over future cash flows is really concerned with the state of information available to the person taking the investment decision. The conditions of certainty refer to a situation where the decision maker has complete information concerning all factors relating to the undertaking of the investment decision. In such a state the decision maker is able to determine precisely the outcome which will arise from any particular action and thus to rank the alternatives and act accordingly. In a situation where information is not complete the outcome of any particular decision cannot be identified precisely. However, while we have only talked about a situation of incomplete information as being uncertainty in the discussion to date, we can actually distinguish between two situations where information is incomplete. The names given to these two states are 'uncertainty' and 'risk'.

With both uncertainty and risk we are considering situations where there are more possible outcomes than will actually occur. In other words, for any particular course of action (e.g. the undertaking of any particular investment opportunity) a range of possible outcomes *may* occur (perhaps depending upon the level of sales achieved, the cost of raw materials, etc.), but, after undertaking the project, only one outcome *will* occur. It is assumed that all possible outcomes can be identified. Where the two states differ, is in relation to information concerning the probability of the occurrence of each possible outcome. A situation of risk refers to a state where the decision maker has sufficient information to determine the probability of each possible outcome occurring. With uncertainty, the decision maker can identify each possible outcome, but does not have the information necessary to determine the probabilities of each of the possibilities. Techniques have been developed to aid investment decision making for both types of situation where there is an absence of certainty.

In considering risk and uncertainty a distinction can be drawn between the absence of certainty over the future earnings of the firm or project and the absence of certainty caused by the way in which a firm or project is financed. The first source of an absence of certainty is known as 'business risk' and the second is known as 'financial risk'.[1] Business risk is caused by the fact that general business conditions, such as the state of demand in the economy, the level of interest rates, the price at which goods can be sold, the behaviour of competitors, the reaction of consumers to the product, etc., are not known with certainty in advance. While estimates of these variables can be given, in reality the estimates are only that and the reality may turn out to be different. Financial risk is associated with the funding of the firm and arises from the fact that while payments to equity holders in the form of dividends do not have to be made if earnings do not warrant such payments, payments to debt holders must be made at the time stipulated in the debt contracts, irrespective of the earnings of the company. Financial risk is the risk that a firm may not be able to meet the financial obligations associated with its debt payments because earnings are insufficient. The higher the proportion of debt in the capital structure of the firm, the greater is the extent of financial risk, other things being equal. While the discussion of risk and uncertainty in this chapter will cover both sources of an absence of certainty, it is business risk which will be given prominence. A fuller discussion of business risk is therefore warranted.

In deriving cash-flow figures to be used in any NPV calculation a great number of estimates will be utilized. For example, for the producer of a new men's fashion product, it will be necessary to have estimates of many factors including: the selling price of the product, the number of sales per period, the cost of materials used in production, the cost of equipment (for example, sewing machines) necessary for production, the production and breakdown rates of such equipment, the labour costs, advertising costs, energy costs, transport costs, factory overheads and many more figures. However, all such estimates are subject to uncertainty or risk.[2] Business risk arises from such uncertainty and the sources of business risk include uncertainty over the level of demand for the product (this could arise from uncertainty over the state of the economy (is it in a good state or is the economy in recession?) or uncertainty over consumer taste in relation to the new product or uncertainty over the behaviour of competitor producers), uncertainty over all costs of production, including output and breakdown rates of machinery, etc. It is variations between estimates of such factors and the reality of such factors which need to be taken into account when dealing with risk and uncertainty in the investment appraisal process.

When faced with risk and uncertainty over so many estimates there may be a tendency to think that cash-flow estimates will be meaningless and that it is not worthwhile undertaking a formal investment appraisal process. Such a course of action is not good managerial practice. While an absence of certainty undoubtedly causes serious problems for the decision maker in arriving at cash-flow estimates, the use of investment appraisal techniques is still valid, and by undertaking a formal investment appraisal process the decision maker is giving him- or herself the best opportunity to take an informed decision. Similarly, while it is necessary to augment the use of investment appraisal techniques with the use of judgement and experience, this does not mean that only judgement and experience should be used. The use of the NPV technique itself, together with the use of some or all of the methods discussed in this chapter and the next, provides important information and insight for the decision maker and makes it more likely that a good decision will be taken.

ATTITUDES TOWARDS RISK

The strengths and weaknesses of the various techniques available for assisting in the decision-making process when there is an absence of certainty are best understood if consideration is first given to the different attitudes which decision makers can have towards risk. Essentially there are three different attitudes which individuals can have towards risk: they can dislike it (i.e. they are risk-averse); they can be indifferent to it (i.e. they are risk-neutral); or they can like it (i.e. they are risk-loving). The different attitudes towards risk can be considered by comparing a certain payoff with a risky payoff. For example, consider a gamble which requires the gambler to pay a sum of money and the payoff from the gamble is determined by the result of tossing a coin. If the toss of the coin yields a head then the payoff is £20. If it yields tails the payoff is £0. Assuming that the coin is 'fair', the expected value of the payoff is £10 (calculated as (£20 × 0.5) + (£0 × 0.5) = £10). A risk-averse individual would not be willing to undertake the gamble if the cost of the gamble is equal to or greater than the expected payoff. In other words, if given a choice between £10 with certainty and the gamble which has an expected payoff of £10 (i.e. an actuarially fair gamble), the risk-averse individual would choose the £10 with certainty. Indeed, a risk-averse individual may not be willing to undertake the gamble even if the cost of the gamble is less than £10, say £9. In this case the individual gains the same level of satisfaction from an amount of money which is certain, but which is below the expected value of the gamble. The more risk-averse is the individual, the lower will have to be the cost of the gamble to make the individual indifferent between the certain amount and the gamble. In contrast, a risk-loving individual would choose the gamble even when the cost of the gamble is £10 or perhaps above this figure, while a risk-neutral individual would be indifferent between £10 with certainty and the gamble.

In practice, the same individual can exhibit risk aversion in some respects and at some times, while displaying risk loving behaviour in relation to other events or at other times. For example, consider an individual who has a house which is worth £100,000 and which has a one in a thousand chance of being burned to the ground. If the house is destroyed by the fire the house will be worth £0. The individual faces a gamble in which the expected value is £99,900 (calculated as (£0 × 0.001) + (£100,000 × 0.999). In such a situation, an individual may demonstrate risk aversion by taking out house insurance which costs £500 and which will pay out £100,000 if the house burns down. The house insurance guarantees the individual will have £99,500 (calculated as £100,000 minus the £500 insurance premium). Even though the certain amount of money is less than the expected value of the gamble the individual is willing to buy the insurance because they are risk-averse with respect to their house burning down. However, at the same time the individual may be willing to gamble on a national lottery where the expected payoff from the gamble is less than the cost of the gamble. Thus at the same time the individual is exhibiting both risk aversion and risk-loving behaviour.

The difference in risk attitudes in the example above is largely due to the amount of money being gambled. With the lottery the stake is small, whereas with the house the stake (potential loss) is considerable. When considering the investments undertaken by firms and the risk attitude to be taken into account in reaching decisions, it is the views of the owners which we should bear in mind. Typically, when individuals invest in firms the investment represents a substantial sum of money for them. They, therefore, typically are risk-averse when it comes to their investments in firms. Thus in undertaking investment appraisal, the decision maker is best advised to work on the basis that the people on whose behalf the decisions are being taken are risk-averse in relation to such decisions.

TECHNIQUES FOR ASSISTING THE DECISION MAKER WHEN FACED WITH RISK AND UNCERTAINTY

There are very many techniques which have been suggested to aid the decision maker who is faced with appraising investments where the future cash flows are not certain. The most simple and intuitive of these will be discussed in this chapter, while the more advanced techniques will be considered in Chapter 6. However, it is worth emphasizing again one important point in relation to decisions where cash flows are not certain. In such a situation there is no 'right answer'. The techniques can only guide the decision maker. Indeed, the different techniques may well provide different guidance. Again, this does not make them invalid. The value of the techniques lies in the fact that they provide the decision maker with useful information and with different ways of thinking about the problems which may arise during the life of the project.

The expected NPV rule

The expected NPV (ENPV) rule is a very simple way of dealing with a situation of risk (it can only be used for such a situation since it requires knowledge of the probabilities of each possible outcome), although its simplicity also results in some major shortcomings. The approach is based on the view that in a situation where cash flows are not known with certainty, it is unwise to base an investment appraisal decision on a single set of cash-flow estimates, relating to one set of assumptions regarding the outcome of the investment (for example, assumptions relating to level of sales, labour costs, raw materials costs, etc.). Rather, the decision maker will make a number of cash-flow estimates based on several scenarios. Consider, for example, a firm which is deciding upon whether to introduce a new range of dining suites. Due to the nature of the business the new line will only have a life of five years. Production of the new line will mainly utilize equipment that the company already owns, but there will be some additional expenditure on equipment and there will be design and advertising costs associated with the new product. The firm believes that the costs associated with production and the level of sales will depend crucially on two factors: the overall state of the economy, which it believes will be either normal or booming, and the reaction of its major competitor, which it believes will either be nothing, or the launch of a new competitive product. On the basis of these two factors there are four possible outcomes: (1) normal economy, no reaction; (2) normal economy, new product launched by rival; (3) booming economy, no reaction; and (4) booming economy, new product launched by rival. The firm calculates the expected cash flows for each of the possible states and the NPV for each state, assuming a discount rate of 12%. The figures are shown in Table 5.1. (Given the nature of the product, the figures should be shown in a table and chairs!)

As a result of its calculations, the firm has four NPV figures rather than only one. Having calculated this range of possible NPV figures, the ENPV approach now requires the firm to calculate an expected value based on its estimates of the probability of each possible state occurring. The firm estimates that the probability of a normal state of the economy occurring is 0.6, while that for the boom is 0.4. The firm also estimates that the probability of its rival not reacting is 0.45, with a 0.55 probability that it will react. Thus, it estimates the probability for each state occurring as follows:

State 1: 0.6 × 0.45 = 0.27.
State 2: 0.6 × 0.55 = 0.33.
State 3: 0.4 × 0.45 = 0.18.
State 4: 0.4 × 0.55 = 0.22.

Table 5.1

Year	State 1	State 2	State 3	State 4
0	−25,500	−25,500	−25,500	−25,500
1	6,000	6,000	9,000	9,000
2	8,000	6,000	12,000	8,500
3	7,500	5,000	12,000	8,000
4	7,000	5,000	12,000	7,500
5	4,000	3,000	7,000	5,000
NPV	−1,709	−6,921	12,242	2,610

Having calculated the probabilities for each possible state, the firm can now calculate an expected value for the NPVs:

ENPV = (−1,709 × 0.27) + (−6,921 × 0.33) + (12,242 × 0.18) + (2,610 × 0.22) = £32.40

It is now possible for the decision maker to come to a decision regarding whether it is worthwhile to undertake this investment, based on the ENPV figure which has been calculated. If the ENPV approach were to be used in a mechanistic manner, the decision rule would be: for independent investments, undertake those investments for which the ENPV is positive and reject those investments which offer a negative ENPV; and for mutually exclusive investments, undertake the project with the highest ENPV, provided that the ENPV is positive. On this basis, the investment project with the cash flows shown in Table 5.1 should be undertaken, as it has a positive ENPV.

However, there are a number of problems associated with the ENPV approach which mean that it should not be used in such a mechanistic fashion, but rather should be used as a guide to the investment decision. The first problem associated with this approach is that it takes no account of attitudes towards risk. Consider, for example, a situation where a choice has to be made between the above investment opportunity and a (mutually exclusive) investment project which offers an NPV figure of £30, whatever the state of the economy and whatever the reaction of competitors. The latter investment has a lower ENPV, yet for many (or possibly most) decision makers, this investment is preferable to the one with the higher ENPV. The reason for this is simple: while the risky investment (with the figures shown in Table 5.1) has a higher ENPV, there is a 0.6 probability (0.27 + 0.33) that this investment will generate a loss. Most risk-averse investors would prefer the £30 with certainty. Thus, by concentrating on only one figure, namely the expected value, the ENPV takes no account of the dispersion around the expected value and thus takes no account of risk or risk attitudes.

A second problem is associated with the nature of expected values. An expected value is a useful concept in a situation where an action is to be repeated on many occasions. For example, if a 'fair' dice is rolled a great many times, then on average any of the six numbers would be expected to be seen one-sixth of the time. In such a situation the concept of expected values is useful. However, if the dice is only to be rolled once, while it is true that each number still has a one-sixth probability of occurring, only one of the numbers will be shown. Here, the concept of expected values is less useful. Similarly, with an investment project which is a 'one-off' and will only be undertaken once, the concept of expected values is less useful. In the example shown in Table 5.1, the expected NPV is £32.40. If the investment were repeated many times, then on average the investment would yield £32.40. However, the investment will only be undertaken once and an NPV of £32.40 will never be realized. Rather, the investment will generate an NPV of (−£1,709) or (−£6,921) or £12,242 or £2,610. Thus, for one-off investments of this type, the ENPV approach is of limited value.

Finally, ENPV suffers from the fact that the forecasting problems associated with any cash-flow figures used in investment appraisal, are increased when more than one scenario is considered. In the above example, it was necessary to estimate cash flows for four different scenarios and to estimate the probability of each of the possible scenarios. Nonetheless, in spite of these shortcomings, the ENPV approach does provide decision makers with important information, provided that the ENPV figure is not used in a mechanistic manner. Of most importance, perhaps, is the fact that the ENPV approach requires the decision maker to consider the possible scenarios which can occur and makes the decision maker investigate the NPV ramifications of each scenario.

The risk-adjusted discount rate approach

This approach to the investment decision-making process is an attempt to deal with the problems caused by an absence of certainty in relation to cash flows in a manner which takes account of the risk attitudes of the decision maker (or more precisely, the risk attitudes of those people on whose behalf the decision is being made, i.e. the owners of the firm). When faced with a situation of risk, investors who are risk-averse will require a higher rate of return to compensate them for taking on that risk. We saw this in the discussion of risk attitudes, when a risk-averse investor would not take on the gamble involving spinning a coin when the expected payoff from the gamble was the same as the cost of the gamble (i.e. when the rate of return was zero). Rather, the risk-averse investor required a positive rate of return to undertake the gamble (for example, if the investor were willing to take on the gamble when the cost of the gamble was £8, then the required rate of return would be 25% (calculated as the expected payoff of the gamble (£10) minus the cost of the gamble (£8), divided by the cost of the gamble (£8). The investor requires a positive rate of return to undertake this investment (i.e. the gamble), even though the payoff is immediate (i.e. even though the investor does not require a rate of return to compensate for the time value of money)).

Thus, risk-averse investors require a higher rate of return to compensate them for the risk they face, and the higher is the level of risk, the greater must be the rate of return. The risk-adjusted rate of return approach puts this simple concept into practice. Decision makers should determine the rate of return which would be required for taking on investments with zero risk (this is the risk-free rate of return or the discount rate to be used when cash flows are known with certainty) and should then add on to this rate of return a risk premium to take account of the riskiness of the investment under consideration. The greater is the degree of risk, the greater should be the risk premium. The rate of return calculated in this way (the risk-free rate plus the risk premium) is then used as the discount rate in the NPV calculation. Lumby points out: 'Thus the risk-adjusted discount rate takes the commonsense approach to handling risk in investment appraisal of adjusting the "height" of the "acceptance hurdle" to correspond to the project's risk level' (1991, p. 275).

It is possible that decision makers determine the discount rate which they believe to be appropriate for each individual investment on a project-by-project basis. Thus, for example, project A is considered and the decision maker decides that the discount rate should be 11%. Similarly, project B is considered and a discount rate of 15% is used, and so on. The problem with such a approach is that determination of the discount rate is left to the subjectiv whims of the decision maker. While such subjectivity cannot be eliminate completely (although a more objective approach will be considered in Chapte 7), the extent to which subjectivity can be introduced can be limited by estab lishing a set of risk categories, before considering any investment opportu nities. An example will help to illustrate this approach.

Example for risk-adjusted discount rates

Before any investments are considered, the decision maker should begin b determining an appropriate discount rate for risk-free investments. Some gui dance on such a rate may be obtained by examining the current rate of retur offered by long-term bonds issued by the government (such bonds can b considered virtually risk-free, since there is almost no possibility of default) Let us suppose that the rate on such bonds is currently 7%. This figure shoul then be used as the base from which discount rates are calculated for risk investments. Having established the required rate of return (discount rate) for risk-free investment, the decision maker should then determine an appropriat classification for all investments which are likely to be considered. For example she may decide that a six-way classification is appropriate, covering the follow ing six types of risk: very low risk; low risk; medium risk; high risk; very high risk; and extremely high risk. The decision maker should then determine the discount rate for each class of risk by choosing an appropriate risk premium fo each class of risk. An example of such a system is given in Table 5.2.

Having undertaken such a classification and determined the discount rate t be used for each class, the decision maker can then consider each investmen opportunity in turn and decide which class they best fit into. This automatically determines the discount rate to be used.

While this approach reduces the opportunity for subjectivity, it does no

Table 5.2

Class of risk	Example of type of project	Risk premium	Discount rate (risk-free rate + risk premium)
Very low	Refunding an issue of corporate bonds	1%	8%
Low	Refurbishment of existing factory	3%	10%
Medium	Increased output of established product	5%	12%
High	Launch of new product	8%	15%
Very high	R&D on areas related to current activity	11%	18%
Extremely high	R&D on completely new areas	15%	22%

Investment Decision Making Under Conditions of Uncertainty: Problems and Simple Solutions

completely remove it. First, unless some formal means is used (such as that discussed in Chapter 7) for determining the appropriate risk premiums, their choice is largely subjective. In addition, a decision maker who is considering a 'pet' project which is, say, extremely high risk, could choose to classify it as medium risk, thus reducing the discount rate and increasing the chance of acceptance of the project. Nonetheless, the approach does force the decision maker to consider discount rates, risk premiums and the nature of the risk of the project being considered and, thus, reduces the opportunity for favouring 'pet' projects.

The use of the risk-adjusted discount rate approach to investment appraisal is, indeed, a common-sense approach, as Lumby suggests. However, there are certain drawbacks associated with the use of the approach which we need to bear in mind when implementing it. The first of these drawbacks has already been mentioned: it has the appearance of objectivity, when, in fact, inherent in the use of the approach is the need for subjectivity, both in the choice of the risk premiums and the assignment of projects to particular risk classes. A second problem arises in situations when considering projects where there are negative net cash flows at some future date. Consider, for example, the firm which has established the classification and discount rates set out in Table 5.2 and which is appraising an extremely risky project which requires an initial investment of £1,000,000, which generates cash inflows of £1,000,000 after one year, £800,000 after two years, £775,000 after three years and which then has a final cash outflow of £1,700,000 in year four (arising, for example, from the need to landscape a site). Using the base (very low risk) discount rate of 8%, the project has an NPV of (−£22,534) and on this basis should not be undertaken. However, the project is extremely risky and the firm, therefore, decides to use a discount rate of 22%. Using this figure, the NPV is +£16,581. Thus, by *increasing* the discount rate, a negative-NPV project has become a positive-NPV project. This is clearly nonsensical.

The reason for the above situation arising is that when there is a large cash outflow late in the life of the project, increasing the discount rate has the effect of decreasing the impact of this cash outflow. Increasing the discount rate to take account of risk only makes sense when dealing with net cash inflows. As far as net cash outflows are concerned, the risk for the firm is that they will be greater than estimated (i.e. greater than £1,700,000, in the above example). Therefore, it does not make sense to reduce the impact of this figure by increasing the discount rate. This problem does not invalidate the risk-adjusted discount rate approach. It simply requires that common sense be used when applying the approach. While it may be advisable to increase the discount rate for risky cash inflows, this should not be done for risky cash outflows.

Sensitivity analysis

Sensitivity analysis is the third and final of the fairly simple traditional approaches to dealing with risk and uncertainty. While it is a relatively simple technique, nonetheless it provides important insights into the nature of the investment under consideration and, importantly, identifies those areas of the investment opportunity which should be of most concern to the decision maker. As the name suggests, the purpose of this approach is to identify those factors to which the 'profitability' of the investment opportunity is most sensitive. Given that information to be input into the investment appraisal process is costly, sensitivity analysis provides important pointers for the decision maker by identifying those areas where efforts should be directed to achieve more reliable data. Thus, the decision maker can expend resources on acquiring information on the most significant factors as far as the 'profitability' of the project is concerned.

To undertake sensitivity analysis the decision maker begins by making the best estimates of the various cash-flow figures which need to be input into the NPV calculation. Clearly, the net cash-flow figures which emerge from this process are made up of a great number of individual estimates, all of which are subject to uncertainty. For example, consider a firm which is appraising an investment opportunity which involves refurbishing a factory it already owns. The factory will be used to produce decorative table lamps (sensitivity analysis is to be used to throw light on the project!). In appraising the investment, cash-flow estimates are required relating to (among other things) total refurbishment costs (including machinery), labour costs, advertising costs, costs of raw materials and sales revenue.[3] In addition, information is required on the discount rate and the life of the investment. The company makes the cash-flow estimates for each item as shown in Table 5.3. The discount rate is estimated to be 10% and the life of the project 8 years.

On the basis of the estimates the net cash flow in year 0 is (−£800,000) and in years 1 to 8 the annual net cash flow is £175,000. Using the standard NPV formula, the firm can calculate the NPV of the project, based on this set of estimates, to be £133,612. Thus, on the basis of these estimates the project appears 'profitable' and one that would be worth pursuing.

The problem, of course, is that figures used in calculating NPV are simply estimates and in reality the cash-flow figures may turn out to be very different from the original estimates. Sensitivity analysis can be used to determine how sensitive the profitability of the project is to the actual cash flows deviating from the estimated figures. With sensitivity analysis each of the figures used in the NPV calculation is examined in turn, to determine how variations from the

Table 5.3

Item	Cash flow estimate (£000)	Year(s) of cash flow
Refurbishment costs	800	0
Labour costs	50	1–8
Advertising costs	20	1–8
Raw materials costs	30	1–8
Sales revenue	275	1–8

Investment Decision Making Under Conditions of Uncertainty: Problems and Simple Solutions

estimated figures impact on the NPV. There are two variations in the use of sensitivity analysis. The first approach we consider examines each item in turn and determines by how much each item can vary before the positive-NPV project becomes a zero-NPV project. In carrying out this examination, all other estimates are held constant at their original level. For example, the NPV of £133,612 will be reduced to zero if the refurbishment costs rise from the estimated £800,000 to £933,612 (all other estimates are assumed to be at their original level). This amounts to a 16.75% increase from the estimated value. This is the margin by which the actual value of the refurbishment costs could be different from estimated without making the project a negative-NPV investment. Having made this calculation we assume that the original estimate of £800,000 is correct and turn our attention to another item, say labour costs. We can calculate that the annual net cash inflow can fall from £175,000 to £150,000 before the project becomes a zero-NPV investment. This means that if all other estimates are correct, labour costs could rise from the estimate of £50,000 per annum to £75,000 per annum without the project having a negative NPV. This represents a margin of 50%. This procedure can then be repeated for each of the other cash-flow figures. The results of this procedure are shown in Table 5.4.

In addition, the discount rate can rise from 10% to 14.43% to reach the break even point, a rise of 44.3%. Similarly, the life of the project would have to fall to approximately six and a half years before the project has a negative NPV, a fall of about 18.75%. These calculations can then be used to identify the cash-flow figures to which the profitability of the project is most sensitive. The figures suggest that sales revenue is most important, followed by refurbishment costs. If sales revenue is 9.1% below estimated then the project is no longer profitable. Similarly, if refurbishment costs are 16.75% above the estimated figure the project will have a zero NPV. Given that the information on which the original estimates were calculated is based on less-than-perfect information and given that information is costly, the decision maker can use the results of the sensitivity analysis to determine in which areas it is most important to gather further information. Thus, in this example, the decision maker might decide to spend more resources on market research to try to get a better estimate of expected sales revenue. In contrast, it does not appear to be particularly worthwhile obtaining more detailed information on labour, advertising or raw materials

Table 5.4

(1) Item	(2) Original cash-flow estimate (£000)	(3) Cash-flow value at which NPV = 0	(4) Percentage change from (2) to (3)
Refurbishment costs	800	934	16.75
Labour costs	50	75	50
Advertising costs	20	45	125
Raw materials costs	30	55	83.33
Sales revenue	275	250	9.1

costs. However, since the profitability of the project is sensitive to the level of refurbishment costs, the decision maker may try to negotiate a contract which makes these costs more certain.

The alternative approach to sensitivity analysis is very similar, but instead of determining the point at which the project breaks even for each item, information is gathered on the impact of a particular variation in each item in turn. For example, the decision maker may feel confident that each of the estimates is fairly accurate, but that the cash flow may vary from the estimated figure by as much as 25%. The decision maker therefore determines the impact of a 25% increase and a 25% decrease in each figure in turn. The results of this analysis are shown in Table 5.5.

The results of this analysis are clearly very similar to the results of the alternative method of sensitivity analysis. The results show that the project no longer remains profitable when there is 25% deviation in the undesirable direction for only three of the estimates. However, in addition, this use of sensitivity analysis gives more information by considering the NPV outcome when the actual figures are better than the estimated figures.

Sensitivity analysis is a very useful means by which to determine the factors to which project profitability is most sensitive. It provides the decision maker with important information on which to base decisions, and, most importantly, provides guidance as to which factors are most worthy of further investigation. However, it is not a panacea to the problems of risk and uncertainty. In particular, while sensitivity analysis provides useful information, in the simple form in which it has been used in the above examples only one factor is varied at a time. In practice, there are likely to be movements in two or more cash-flow figures at the same time. For example, rising interest rates may lead to an increase in the discount rate and, through their impact on household disposable income, a fall in sales revenue. It is important that such interrelationships are given consideration when the approach is being used.

Table 5.5

(1) Item	(2) Original estimate	(3) NPV for 25% increase in item	(4) NPV for 25% decrease in item
Refurbishment costs	£800,000	−£66,388	£333,612
Labour costs	£50,000	£66,926	£200,299
Advertising costs	£20,000	£106,937	£160,287
Raw materials costs	£30,000	£93,600	£173,624
Sales revenue	£275,000	£500,389	−£233,164
Discount rate	10%	£54,358	£225,028
Life of project	8 years	£275,299	−£37,829
Baseline NPV	133,612		

Risk and uncertainty are features of almost any investment opportunity. As such the decision maker should ensure that account is taken of their potential impact on the investment under consideration and should also take into account the sources of risk and uncertainty and the risk attitudes of the individuals on whose behalf the investment decision is being made. This chapter has provided an introduction to the issues of risk and uncertainty and has set out some simple techniques which have been developed for assisting the decision maker facing investments which have cash flows which are not known with certainty. The next chapter will examine more advanced techniques for dealing with risk and uncertainty. The key points from this chapter are as follows:

- The techniques available to the decision maker under conditions of risk and uncertainty all take as their starting point the NPV method. Developments of this method are utilized when dealing with this feature of investment opportunities.
- Conditions of certainty refer to a situation where the decision maker has complete information concerning all factors relating to the undertaking of the investment decision.
- With both uncertainty and risk we are considering situations where there are more possible outcomes than will actually occur. Where risk and uncertainty differ is in relation to information concerning the probability of the occurrence of each possible outcome.
- A situation of risk refers to a state where the decision maker has sufficient information to determine the probability of each possible outcome occurring.
- In a situation of uncertainty, the decision maker can identify each possible outcome, but does not have the information necessary to determine the probabilities of each of the possibilities.
- A distinction can be drawn between the absence of certainty over the future earnings of the firm or project and the absence of certainty caused by the way in which a firm or project is financed. The first source of an absence of certainty is known as 'business risk' and the second is known as 'financial risk'.
- Business risk is caused by the fact that general business conditions, such as the state of demand in the economy, the level of interest rates, the price at which goods can be sold, the behaviour of competitors, the reaction of consumers to the product, etc., are not known with certainty in advance.
- Financial risk is the risk that a firm may not be able to meet the financial obligations associated with its debt payments because earnings are insufficient.
- When faced with risk and uncertainty, the decision maker should take account of the risk attitudes of the person on whose behalf the investment decision is being taken.

- Individuals can be risk-averse, risk-neutral or risk-loving. In general, in considering investments within firms it is sensible to assume that the owners are risk-averse with respect to such decisions. As such they will require a higher rate of return, the higher is the risk of a project.
- The expected NPV (ENPV) rule is a very simple way of dealing with a situation of risk. The approach is based on the view that in a situation where cash flows are not known with certainty, it is unwise to base an investment appraisal decision on a single set of cash-flow estimates. Rather the decision maker will make a number of cash-flow estimates based on several scenarios and calculate the expected value of the NPVs under each such scenario.
- The risk-adjusted discount rate approach puts into practice the concept that the greater the risk of the investment, the higher must be the rate of return. With this approach, the decision makers should determine the discount rate which would be required for taking on investments with zero risk and should then add on to this rate a risk premium to take account of the riskiness of the investment under consideration.
- Sensitivity analysis can be used to determine how sensitive the profitability of the project is to the actual cash flows deviating from the estimated figures. With sensitivity analysis each of the figures used in the NPV calculation is examined in turn, to determine how variations from the estimated figures impact on the NPV.
- All of these simple techniques provide important information to the decision maker, but they all suffer from shortcomings. It is therefore important that the techniques are not used as decision rules.
- When faced with risk and uncertainty there may be a tendency to think that it is not worthwhile undertaking a formal investment appraisal process. Such a course of action is not good managerial practice. By undertaking a formal investment appraisal process the decision maker is given the opportunity to take an informed decision.
- This is further enhanced by utilizing the techniques which have been developed for assisting decision making under conditions of risk and uncertainty and which have been discussed in this chapter.

WORKED EXAMPLES

5.1 A company is considering launching a new product and believes that the success of the project will depend upon the state of the economy over the next few years. It estimates that there are three likely states of the economy (boom, neutral and recession), and that the product will have a life of four years. On this basis, it estimates the net cash flows (NCFs) shown in the table.

Year	NCFs – boom (£s)	NCFs – neutral (£s)	NCFs – recession (£s)
0	−60,000	−60,000	−60,000
1	25,000	20,000	15,000
2	25,000	20,000	15,000
3	25,000	20,000	15,000
4	25,000	20,000	15,000

The likelihood of each state of the economy occurring is estimated to be: boom: 0.2; neutral: 0.5; recession: 0.3

(a) Calculate the NPV for each state of the economy, assuming a discount rate of 12%.

(b) Calculate the ENPV of the project.

Answer:

(a) We can use the present-value-of-an-annuity table at the back of the book to determine the discount factor for an annuity of £1 paid for four years, when the discount rate is 12%. From Table B we can see that the appropriate discount factor is 3.03735. We can now calculate the NPV under each state of the economy:

$$NPV_{Boom} = 25,000 \times 3.03735 - 60,000 = £15,934,$$
$$NPV_{Neutral} = 20,000 \times 3.03735 - 60,000 = £747,$$
$$NPV_{Recession} = 15,000 \times 3.03735 - 60,000 = (-£14,440).$$

(b) We can now calculate the ENPV:

$$ENPV = 0.2 \times 15,934 + 0.5 \times 747 + 0.3 \times (-14,440) = -£771.7.$$

5.2 A firm is undertaking an investment appraisal for a new product and estimates the main components of the cash flows over the 6 year life of the project to be as in the table.

Item	Cash-flow estimate (£000)	Year(s) of cash flow
Cost of refitting factory	1,000	0
Costs of new machinery	400	0
Labour costs	60	1–6
Advertising costs	25	1–6
Raw materials costs	35	1–6
Energy costs	15	1–6
Sales revenue	535	1–6

The discount rate is 16%.

(a) Calculate the NPV of the project.

(b) Determine the value of the NPV when each of the estimated figures is varied (one at a time) by +25% and −25%. Assume that the life of the project is fixed.

Answers:

On the basis of these estimates, the net cash flow in year 0 is (−£1,400,000) and in years 1–6 the annual net cash flow is £400,000.

(a) From table B, the discount factor for an annuity of £1 for six years when the discount rate is 16% is 3.68474. The NPV of the project is:

$$NPV = 400,000 \times 3.68474 - 1,400,000 = £73,896.$$

(b) We begin by calculating the cash flows when they are 25% higher or 25% lower than the original estimate, as shown in the table.

Item	Original cash-flow estimate (£000)	Cash-flow estimate increased by 25% (£000)	Cash-flow estimate decreased by 25% (£000)
Cost of refitting factory	1,000	1,250	750
Costs of new machinery	400	500	300
Labour costs	60	75	45
Advertising costs	25	31.25	18.75
Raw materials costs	35	43.75	26.25
Energy costs	15	18.75	11.25
Sales revenue	535	668.75	401.25
Discount rate	16%	20%	12%

We can now calculate the NPV for the project when all estimates are as they were originally, except for the cost of refitting the factory. The cash inflows in each year are unchanged, but with a 25% increase in this cost the NPV falls by £250,000 to (−£176,104). Similarly if the cost of refitting is 25% below the estimate, the NPV is £323,896. On the same basis, variations in the cost of new machinery of +25% lead to an NPV of (−£26,104), while a 25% reduction in this cost leads to an NPV of £173,896. A 25% increase in labour costs reduces the annual net cash flow by £15,000. Thus the NPV is:

$$NPV = 385,000 \times 3.68474 - £1,400,000 = £18,625.$$

Undertaking similar analysis for each of the estimates allows us to generate the figures in the table.

Item	Original cash-flow estimate (£000)	NPV when cash-flow estimate increased by 25% (£)	NPV when cash-flow estimate decreased by 25% (£)
Cost of refitting factory	1,000	−176,104	323,896
Costs of new machinery	400	−26,104	173,896
Labour costs	60	18,625	129,167
Advertising costs	25	50,866	96,926
Raw materials costs	35	41,655	106,137
Energy costs	15	60,078	87,714
Sales revenue	535	566,730	−418,938
Discount rate	16%	−69,796	244,564

QUESTIONS

5.1 Distinguish between risk and uncertainty.

5.2 What is the difference between business risk and financial risk?

5.3 Explain the three different attitudes to risk. Make use of an actuarially fair gamble to illustrate your answer.

5.4 Outline the main problems associated with the use of the ENPV approach.

5.5 Explain the principle underlying the risk-adjusted discount rate approach. Why might the use of a higher discount rate to reflect increased risk be unwise in some circumstances?

5.6 Why is sensitivity analysis of assistance to decision makers appraising investment opportunities?

NOTES

1 While we typically distinguish between risk and uncertainty in terms of knowledge about probabilities of the possible outcomes, when we discuss the sources of risk and uncertainty it is usual to talk in terms of risk only. This reflects an inconsistency in terminology, rather than any decision on whether probabilities are or are not known.

2 While the distinction has been made between risk and uncertainty, in the remainder of the book the two terms will be used interchangeably to avoid unnecessary repitition, unless the distinction is important in the particular context.

3 In practice there are likely to be many more estimates required. However, the ones given here will suffice for illustrating the approach based on sensitivity analysis.

6 INVESTMENT DECISION MAKING UNDER CONDITIONS OF UNCERTAINTY: MORE ADVANCED SOLUTIONS

Introduction

In the previous chapter we identified the problems which can arise when the cash flows associated with an investment project are not known with certainty, drew a distinction between risk and uncertainty, and considered the main sources of risk and uncertainty. In addition, we established that while different investors may have different attitudes towards risk, when considering investment opportunities decision makers would be well advised to work on the basis that the people on whose behalf the decision is being taken are risk-averse. Finally, consideration was given to some simple, *ad hoc*, means for addressing problems caused by an absence of certainty.

In this chapter we consider other means by which the difficulties arising from uncertainty can be tackled. The techniques we consider in this chapter are more advanced than those considered so far. However, while the methods to be discussed here are less simplistic, we still need to remember that the use of these techniques will not provide hard-and-fast decision rules. The proviso made in the last chapter continues to hold. In a situation of risk and uncertainty, different approaches to considering the investment decision problem inform and provide insight into the decision making process, but they do not provide definitive answers and they do not replace the decision making process. It is still necessary to augment the use of these techniques with the use of judgement and experience. Three approaches will be discussed in this chapter: decision trees; simulation; and game-theoretic. The first two of these build on the *ad hoc* techniques discussed previously. The third provides a very different way by which to address the problems of risk and uncertainty.

Decision tree analysis builds on the basic concept we considered when discussing the ENPV approach in the previous chapter. We saw with that approach that in a situation where cash flows are not known with certainty, investment appraisal decisions would not be based on a single set of cash flow estimates, relating to one set of assumptions. Rather management would make a number of cash flow estimates relating to different scenarios. However, with the ENPV example used in Chapter 5 we assumed that whichever of the four different possible scenarios occurred, the firm would be faced with that scenario for the remainder of the life of the project. To recapitulate, the example in Chapter 5 was concerned with a firm which is deciding upon whether to introduce a new range of dining suites which would have a life of five years. The firm believes that the cash flows of the project will be determined by the overall state of the economy, which it believes will be either normal or booming, and the reaction of its major competitor, which it believes will be either none or the launch of a new competitive product. On the basis of these two factors there are four possible outcomes: (1) normal economy, no reaction; (2) normal economy, new product launched by rival; (3) booming economy, no reaction; and (4) booming economy, new product launched by rival. The table of cash flows for each possible state which was shown in Chapter 5 is repeated here as Table 6.1 for convenience. The discount rate is 12%.

In this example, the only difference between state 1 and state 3 relates to whether the economy is in a neutral state or is booming. However, it is assumed that if the economy is in a neutral state in year 1 it will remain in a normal state for the whole life of the project. Likewise, if the economy is booming in year 1 it will be booming for the whole five-year period. Similar assumptions are made about competitor reactions.

In practice, of course, not only is the environment in which firms operate uncertain, but it is also dynamic. For example, while the economy may be in a normal state in year 1, it is quite possible that it will then be in a boom state in year 2 and return to a normal state in years 3 and 4, before returning to a boom state. At the time when the investment decision is being taken, it is clearly not known what pattern the economy will take over the next few years, but it is

Table 6.1

Year	State 1	State 2	State 3	State 4
0	−25,500	−25,500	−25,500	−25,500
1	6,000	6,000	9,000	9,000
2	8,000	6,000	12,000	8,500
3	7,500	5,000	12,000	8,000
4	7,000	5,000	12,000	7,500
5	4,000	3,000	7,000	5,000
NPV	−1,709	−6,921	12,242	2,610

fairly certain that it will not be the same in each year. It is therefore desirable to refine the ENPV approach to take account of the dynamic nature of the environment in which firms operate. The decision tree approach provides just such a refinement.

The decision tree approach will be examined by making use of the above example, but now allowing the state of the economy to change on a year-by-year basis. To keep the analysis relatively simple it will be assumed that the only variable which affects the NPV of the project is the state of the economy. It will be assumed that competitors do not respond to the new product. Thus the cash-flow forecasts which are of relevance here are those shown for states 1 and 3 in Table 6.1. The analysis detailed below could be extended to take account of the possibility of such a reaction, but consideration of this issue is unnecessary for illustrating the principles of the decision tree approach.

Let us again assume that the firm estimates the probabilities of the two possible states of the economy. However, we will now assume that the probability of there being a boom next year is affected by the state of the economy this year. If the state of the economy this year is in neutral, then the firm estimates that there is a 0.9 chance that the state of the economy will be neutral in the following year, while the probability of the economy booming in the following year is estimated to be only 0.1. However, if the economy is booming this year the probability of there being another boom next year increases to 0.4, while the probability of the economy being in a neutral state next year is 0.6. Let us also assume that in the year when the investment is undertaken the firm knows that the economy will be in a neutral state. Thus in the first year of the project there is a 90% chance that the cash flow will be £6,000 and a 10% chance it will be £9,000. In the second year the cash flow will be either £8,000 or £12,000, but now the probability of each possible outcome will depend on whether the economy was booming or in neutral in year 1. If the economy was in neutral in year 1, then the chance of its being in neutral again in year 2 is 0.9. However, if the economy is booming in year 1, then the probability of its being in neutral in year 2 is only 0.6. This process carries through for the remaining years. Since the state of the economy can change from year to year there are now a whole range of possible cash-flow patterns and associated probabilities. These are shown in the decision tree in Figure 6.1. Present values and probabilities for any particular state are calculated by following a particular set of branches of the tree. The tree shows, for example, that the probability of the economy booming in each of the five years of the life of the project is 2.56% (0.0256, the first probability figure which is calculated as (0.1 × 0.4 × 0.4 × 0.4 × 0.4)). The present value of the project when the economy is booming each year is £12,241.60, the same as in column 3 of Table 6.1. Similarly, by following the relevant branches of the tree, we can see that if the economy is in neutral in year 1, booms in year 2, is in neutral in years 3 and 4, and booms again in year 5, the series of cash flows from the project will be £6,000, £12,000, £7,500, £7,000 and £7,000, the present value of this cash-flow series will be £3,182.40 and the probability of this occurring will be 0.00486 (calculated as (0.9 × 0.1 × 0.6 × 0.9 × 0.1)). The final column of the figure gives the expected value which is calculated as PV × probability.

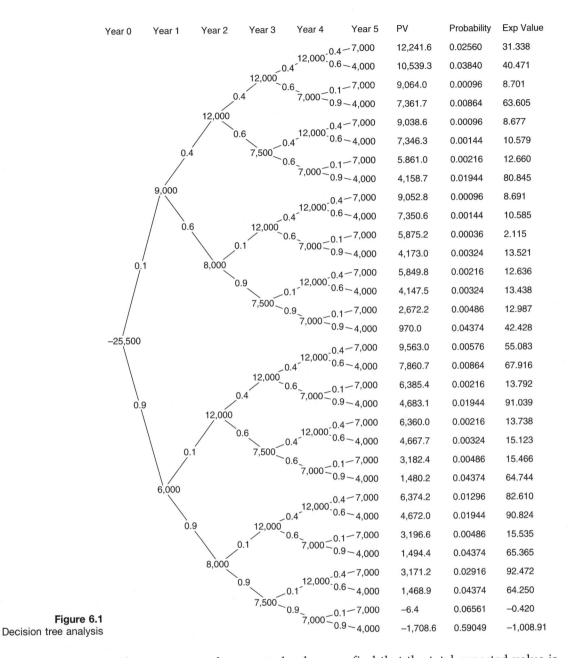

Year 0	Year 1	Year 2	Year 3	Year 4	Year 5	PV	Probability	Exp Value
					0.4—7,000	12,241.6	0.02560	31.338
				12,000 0.6—4,000	10,539.3	0.03840	40.471
				0.1—7,000	9,064.0	0.00096	8.701
				7,000 0.9—4,000	7,361.7	0.00864	63.605
				0.4—7,000	9,038.6	0.00096	8.677
				12,000 0.6—4,000	7,346.3	0.00144	10.579
				0.1—7,000	5,861.0	0.00216	12.660
				7,000 0.9—4,000	4,158.7	0.01944	80.845
				0.4—7,000	9,052.8	0.00096	8.691
				12,000 0.6—4,000	7,350.6	0.00144	10.585
				0.1—7,000	5,875.2	0.00036	2.115
				7,000 0.9—4,000	4,173.0	0.00324	13.521
				0.4—7,000	5,849.8	0.00216	12.636
				12,000 0.6—4,000	4,147.5	0.00324	13.438
				0.1—7,000	2,672.2	0.00486	12.987
				7,000 0.9—4,000	970.0	0.04374	42.428
				0.4—7,000	9,563.0	0.00576	55.083
				12,000 0.6—4,000	7,860.7	0.00864	67.916
				0.1—7,000	6,385.4	0.00216	13.792
				7,000 0.9—4,000	4,683.1	0.01944	91.039
				0.4—7,000	6,360.0	0.00216	13.738
				12,000 0.6—4,000	4,667.7	0.00324	15.123
				0.1—7,000	3,182.4	0.00486	15.466
				7,000 0.9—4,000	1,480.2	0.04374	64.744
				0.4—7,000	6,374.2	0.01296	82.610
				12,000 0.6—4,000	4,672.0	0.01944	90.824
				0.1—7,000	3,196.6	0.00486	15.535
				7,000 0.9—4,000	1,494.4	0.04374	65.365
				0.4—7,000	3,171.2	0.02916	92.472
				12,000 0.6—4,000	1,468.9	0.04374	64.250
				0.1—7,000	−6.4	0.06561	−0.420
				7,000 0.9—4,000	−1,708.6	0.59049	−1,008.91

Figure 6.1
Decision tree analysis

If we now sum the expected values we find that the total expected value is £111.90 and the project appears profitable. However, if the firm had undertaken a simple ENPV calculation on the assumption that whatever state occurred in the first year would continue throughout the five-year period, then the ENPV would have been −£313.90 (calculated as (−£1,709 × 0.9) + (£12,242 × 0.1)) and the assumption would incorrectly have been made that there was a 90% chance of the economy not booming at any time during the life of the project. The decision tree analysis gives a more accurate picture. Not only is the ENPV positive when the simplifying assumption regarding the state of the economy is not made, but also, as can be seen from the last row of the table, the probability that the economy is in neutral throughout the life of the project is below 60%, rather than the 90% that might otherwise have been assumed.

A similar analysis could be carried out if the economy were booming when the project was undertaken. This would yield an ENPV of £1,318.85, compared to the simple ENPV value of £3,871.40 when the assumption is made that the economy will be booming throughout the life of the project (calculated as (£12,242 × 0.4) + (−£1,709 × 0.6)). Such analysis would show that there is only about a 10% chance that the economy will be booming throughout the life of the project, rather than the 40% chance implicitly assumed in the simple analysis. Thus, it can be seen that the use of decision tree analysis can provide decision makers with considerably more insight into the profitability or otherwise of a project than can the use of simple ENPV.

SIMULATION MODELS

In discussing sensitivity analysis in Chapter 5 we saw that while the approach provides important information regarding which variables in the investment decision are of greatest importance in terms of project profitability, it suffers from the shortcoming that it only gives consideration to movements in one variable at a time. As mentioned in the previous chapter, in practice there are likely to be movements in two or more variables at the same time. Simulation techniques avoid this shortcoming by allowing the evaluation of changes in several variables simultaneously. However, since simulation methods can only be satisfactorily adopted with the use of computers, such an approach is most appropriate when considering relatively large projects. Indeed, given that the actual use of simulation techniques is relatively complex, only a brief description will be given here.

A simulation model is a means by which a mathematical model is used to simulate the possible outcomes of a financial decision. In discussing sensitivity analysis we began by providing a 'best guess' estimate of each variable in the cash flow forecast (for example, labour costs, advertising costs, sales revenue etc.). With simulation techniques it is not sufficient to provide only one cash-flow estimate for each variable. Rather, it is necessary to identify a probability distribution for the outcome for each variable. For example, in the sensitivity analysis example in Table 5.3 the estimate of labour costs was £50,000 per annum. While this may be the mean or expected value of annual labour costs, in reality there is a whole distribution of possible outcomes for this variable, with each possible outcome having a particular probability of occurring. Figure 6.2 shows an example of such a distribution (a normal distribution with a mean of £50,000).

Just as there is a probability distribution of possible outcomes for labour costs, so too will there be a probability distribution of outcomes for all other

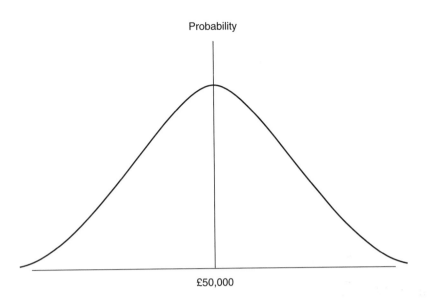

Probability

£50,000

Figure 6.2
A normal distribution with a
mean of £50,000

variables in the cash-flow forecasts for the investment decision. Simulation analysis begins by stipulating the probability distribution for each variable and inputting this data into a computer simulation model. The model is then run with the computer selecting at random an outcome for each variable from the probability distribution for that variable. For example, using and extending the example in Table 5.3, the model may select figures of £825,000 for refurbishment costs, £52,500 for labour costs, £18,000 for advertising costs, £37,000 for raw material costs and £320,000 for sales revenue. On the basis of these selections a figure for NPV will be calculated. The model is then run a number of times more to get a large number of NPV figures (running the model 100 times or more is not unusual). Each time the model is run is known as an 'iteration'. The results of the large number of iterations are then used to plot a probability distribution for the project's NPV. Figure 6.3 shows an example of such a probability distribution (a normal distribution for NPV with mean of £133,000).

The simulation approach has a number of advantages. First, rather than only having one figure for the NPV (for example, a mean figure) we now have an entire probability distribution for the NPV. This allows the decision maker to obtain answers to particular questions about the project. For example, the decision maker can ask 'What is the probability that the project will have a negative NPV?', or if a limited loss is bearable but a large loss is not, 'What is the probability that the NPV will be below (−£15,000)?' A second advantage of this approach is that the very process of setting up the problem on the computer requires the decision maker to gain a good understanding of the cash flows associated with the project and their respective probabilities. Also, by providing information not only on a mean value, but also on the standard deviation of the distribution, it allows a more explicit consideration of the risk–return trade-off. Finally, the approach explicitly recognizes the interrelationships which exist between the different variables.

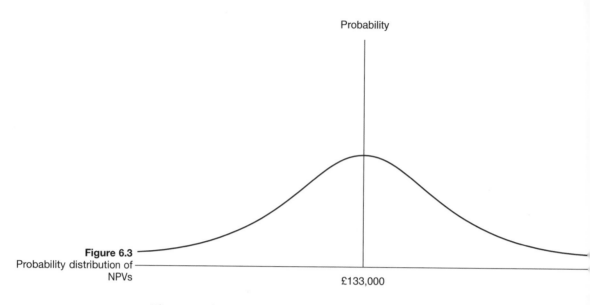

Figure 6.3
Probability distribution of
NPVs

£133,000

The main disadvantage of the approach is that it can be very time consuming and very costly to gather the necessary information and to input the data into the simulation model. In addition, it is not easy to identify the probability distributions for each variable, especially if the project is new and a 'one-off'. It is also the case that there may be complex interrelationships between variables which make identifying and formulating an appropriate model even more complex. For example, the sales revenue may be partly determined by the advertising costs incurred. If this is the case, then ideally the model should be capable of dealing with this interrelationship. Nonetheless, in spite of these problems, the method may be an appropriate means by which to consider investment decisions if they involve a large capital outlay. However, as always, the decision maker needs to consider the costs of implementing such a model and the necessity for good-quality information to be input into the model.

GAME-THEORETIC APPROACHES

In relation to this set of approaches to the investment decision, it is perhaps worthwhile to begin by stating that while they are based on game theory, these approaches are relatively simple to understand. Game-theoretic approaches to investment decision making are concerned with situations where the decision maker has no knowledge of the probabilities of each possible outcome. In other words, they are appropriate to decision making under conditions of uncertainty, rather than conditions of risk. Five approaches which fall within this general category will be considered for assisting the decision maker faced with an investment under uncertainty: (i) the *Bayes–Laplace* criterion; (ii) the *maximax* criterion; (iii) the *maximin* criterion; (iv) the *Hurwicz* criterion; and (v) the

Investment Decision Making under Conditions of Uncertainty: More Advanced Solutions

minimax regret criterion. It is helpful to demonstrate the use of these approaches by applying them to an example. The following example will be used to illustrate all five approaches.

Example for game-theoretic approaches

Datadate plc is a company with an established product in the electronic diary and organizer market. Its product is highly priced and aimed at the upper end of the executive market. Its manager, Ms April Noone, is now considering new strategies for the next ten years and is faced with four mutually exclusive options:

Option A: the firm can stay in the same niche market, but increase advertising to try to take a bigger share of the market;

Option B: the firm can bring out a cheaper version of the existing product at a lower price and increase sales revenue by moving down market;

Option C: the firm can add additional functions to the existing product, charge a much higher price for the 'special' version of the product and try to sell the product up-market, while maintaining its existing standard product; and

Option D: stop producing the standard product, but sell the 'special' as a new product in its existing market.

The firm believes that the profitability of the different options will depend on the level of demand for the product. In turn this will depend on the state of the economy (in recession, neutral or booming) and the reaction of competitor firms (competitor firms will either have no reaction or, if the economy is in neutral or booming, may launch a rival product). As a result, Ms Noone believes that there will be five different possible levels of demand determined as follows:

D1: economy in recession, no reaction from competitors;
D2: economy in neutral, no reaction from competitors;
D3: economy in neutral, competitors launch new rival product;
D4: economy booming, no reaction from competitors:
D5: economy booming, competitors launch new rival product.

She estimates the NPV of each of the four options under each possible level of demand. Table 6.2 shows the NPV of each option for each level of demand.

Table 6.2 NPV with different options and different levels of demand

Demand Option	D1	D2	D3	D4	D5
A	−£1,500	−£250	−£575	+£2,350	+£770
B	−£750	+£225	−£975	+£2,000	+£500
C	−£235	£0	−£175	+£950	+£400
D	−£100	+£100	−£200	+£500	+£300

Faced with the range of possible outcomes and having no knowledge of the probability of each possible outcome, Ms Noone has no obvious means by which to reach a decision on which investment alternative to undertake. A first step would be to consider whether one alternative dominates the others in terms of NPV under all scenarios. However, a quick examination of the table shows that this is not the case. For example, if D1 occurs then alternative D provides the highest NPV (albeit that it is a negative value). However, if D2 occurs B is superior. Thus no alternative is superior in all situations and the decision as to which option to undertake is non-trivial. Similarly, the decision maker should consider whether one alternative is always dominated by another. If there is, then that alternative can be ruled out. For example, consider a fifth option (E) which offers NPVs under the five possible outcomes of −£850, +£200, −£1,000, +£1,780 and +£450. It can be seen that option E is dominated by option B. Whichever level of demand occurs option B offers a higher NPV than option E. Thus option E could be ruled out as B is clearly superior. Of the four options shown in the table, none is dominated by any other under all possible levels of demand. Thus, each of the four alternatives should remain under consideration.

Given that no option is clearly superior under all levels of demand, Ms Noone must find another criterion for making a decision. The five approaches mentioned above will now be considered in turn. These five approaches provide the decision maker with means by which to consider the options. They do not provide the decision maker with definitive advice, but do provide important information and insights. However, it is quite possible that the five criteria will give conflicting advice.

(i) The Bayes–Laplace criterion

It has already been stated that the decision maker is faced with uncertainty and so has no knowledge of the probabilities of each of the possible outcomes. In this situation the Bayes–Laplace criterion states that the decision maker should assign equal probabilities to each possible outcome. These probabilities can then be used as the basis for calculating an ENPV figure. For example, in the case shown above in Table 6.2 there are five possible outcomes for the level of demand. Therefore, if the Bayes–Laplace criterion is used a probability of 0.2 should be applied to each possible outcome. Similarly, if there had been eight possible outcomes a probability of 0.125 would be attached to each possible outcome. Using probabilities of 0.2 for each possible outcome it is straightforward to calculate the ENPV of each option:

ENPV (A) = (0.2 × (−1,500)) + (0.2 × (−250)) + (0.2 × (−575)) + (0.2 × 2,350) + (0.2 × 770)
    = £159,
ENPV (B) = (0.2 × (−750)) + (0.2 × 225) + (0.2 × (−975)) + (0.2 × 2,000) + (0.2 × 500)
    = £200,
ENPV (C) = (0.2 × (−235)) + (0.2 × 0) + (0.2 × (−175)) + (0.2 × 950) + (0.2 × 400)
    = £188,
ENPV (D) = (0.2 × (−100)) + (0.2 × 100) + (0.2 × (−200)) + (0.2 × 500) + (0.2 × 300)
    = £120.

On the basis of these ENPV calculations Ms Noone would choose *option B*. While the notion that in the absence of probability information it is sensible to assume each outcome is equally likely may appear warranted, this approach to investment decision making has some shortcomings. First, it suffers from the problems already discussed in relation to the ENPV approach. In particular, it takes no account of the decision maker's attitude towards risk or that of the owners. For example, while option B has the highest ENPV, the owners may view option C or D more favourably, given that the potential loss is much smaller than that for B. Second, while the decision maker may be able to identify the outcomes that she believes are most likely (for example, the five levels of demand), it is unlikely that she will be aware of all possible outcomes. For example, it is possible that competitors will launch a rival product even if the economy is in recession. Such a possibility is not considered in Table 6.2. Similarly, the possible outcomes for option A are assumed only to depend on the state of the economy and the reaction of competitors. However, in reality the success of the advertising campaign and the effect of similar campaigns by rivals will also determine the NPV of the project. Thus, in practice there are likely to be many more possible outcomes than those identified in the table. If there are ten such outcomes, then the probability assigned to each under the Bayes–Laplace criterion should be 0.1. Since the decision maker has only identified five of the possible outcomes, the probability attached to each identified outcome is clearly greater than it should be.

(ii) The maximax criterion

The maximax approach to investment decision making is based on the view that the decision maker is of an optimistic disposition. It involves only giving consideration to one possible outcome for each option: the outcome to be considered is the best possible outcome. Essentially, the decision maker is working on the assumption that once she has made a decision the best possible result will occur. Thus, the decision maker should choose the maximum of the maximums. The maximum NPV for each option is as follows:

A: +£2,350,
B: +£2,000,
C: +£950,
D: +£500.

The highest of these best possible outcomes is +£2,350 for *option A* and it is this option which would be chosen by the maximax criterion.

In the example in Table 6.2, the best possible outcome for each option is D4 (i.e. where the economy is booming and competitors do not launch a new product). In other cases it is possible that for some alternatives the best possible outcome will occur for different options under different states of the world. For example, it is quite possible that for an option F, the NPV figures are −£300, £700, −£100, £500 and £200. In this case the best possible outcome occurs under level of demand D2. However, the choice is simply based on the best of the bests. Thus the best figure of +£700 for F would be compared with that for A, and A would thus be chosen.

The problem with this approach is that it only considers one possible payoff for each option. Thus, it does not take account of the dispersion of possible payoffs and therefore does not take account of the decision maker's attitude towards risk. For example, while A offers the highest possible NPV it also offers the possibility of the highest possible loss if the level of demand turns out to be D1.

(iii) The maximin criterion

With this approach the outlook of the decision maker is the opposite of that for the maximax approach. Here the decision maker is assumed to be pessimistic and believes that whatever decision is taken the worst possible outcome will occur. The decision maker therefore examines each option and identifies the worst possible outcome. She then chooses that option which has the maximum of the minimum NPV figures. The worst possible outcome for each option is as follows:

A: −£1,500,
B: −£975,
C: −£235,
D: −£200.

Clearly, the maximum of these minimum NPV figures is −£200 for *option D*. Therefore, using this criterion option D would be undertaken.

As with the maximax approach the maximin criterion suffers from the fact that it only gives consideration to one possible outcome for each option. It may be a useful approach in particular circumstances, for example, where a firm is in a very precarious financial position and a large loss could lead to the firm having to cease trading. However, by focusing on only one possible outcome it is conservative in the extreme. For example, while D has the maximum of the minimums, option C is only marginally worse by this criterion and yet offers the potential for much higher payoffs. Indeed, using the Bayes–Laplace criterion it has been seen that option C has a much higher ENPV figure than does option D.

(iv) The Hurwicz criterion

The Hurwicz criterion attempts to take account of both optimistic and pessimistic attitudes by suggesting that a weighted average be calculated of the best possible payoff for each option and the worst possible payoff for each option. The option with the largest weighted average would then be chosen. The choice of the weights to be attached to the two outcomes will be determined by the decision maker to reflect her attitude and beliefs. For example, a particularly risk-averse investor might give a weight of only 0.2 to the best possible outcome and one of 0.8 to the worst possible outcome. In contrast, a more optimistic or less risk-averse investor might apply weights of 0.45 and 0.55. The weights chosen will clearly determine which option is chosen. For example, if weights of 0.2 (for best) and 0.8 (for worst) are applied the weighted payoff figures are as follows:

$$A: (0.2 \times £2,350) + [0.8 \times (-£1,500)] = -£730,$$
$$B: (0.2 \times £2,000) + [0.8 \times (-£975)] = -£380,$$
$$C: (0.2 \times £950) + [0.8 \times (-£235)] = +£2,$$
$$D: (0.2 \times £500) + [0.8 \times (-£200)] = -£60.$$

On this basis *option C* would be chosen. On the other hand, if weights of 0.45 and 0.55 are used the weighted payoffs are as follows:

$$A: (0.45 \times £2,350) + [0.55 \times (-£1,500)] = +£232.5,$$
$$B: (0.45 \times £2,000) + [0.55 \times (-£975)] = +£363.75,$$
$$C: (0.45 \times £950) + [0.55 \times (-£235)] = +£298.25,$$
$$D: (0.45 \times £500) + [0.55 \times (-£200)] = +£115.$$

On the basis of these weights *option B* would be chosen. The fact that the same criterion can lead to different options being chosen when the weights are varied highlights one of the apparent problems of this approach. However, with the Hurwicz criterion the choice of weights should reflect the risk attitude of the decision maker. Thus the same decision maker should not be using two or more different sets of weights. However, a further problem remains. While the Hurwicz criterion has the advantage over the two previous approaches that it does not only consider one possible outcome, nonetheless, it still does not consider all possible outcomes. The intermediate outcomes are given no consideration at all with this criterion.

(v) The minimax regret criterion

The previous three approaches to decision making under conditions of uncertainty simply concentrate on the possible outcomes and how optimistic or pessimistic the decision maker is feeling at the time the project is chosen. The minimax regret criterion involves a more elaborate approach in which the decision maker gives consideration to how she will feel after having made a choice and the actual outcome has become known. Thus consideration is given to the opportunity cost associated with a decision being taken which turns out to be less than optimal. After having made a less than optimal choice as to which option to undertake Ms Noone will feel that she has incurred a loss, or will feel 'regret'. The idea behind the minimax regret approach is for the decision maker to choose the option which will minimize the maximum regret that the decision maker will feel for each option. In order to implement this criterion it is first of all necessary to create a new table, a 'regret table', which shows the amount of regret that Ms Noone will feel for each option under each possible outcome.

To illustrate how the regret table is constructed consider the example where the decision maker chooses option A and the level of demand turns out to be D1. The NPV of A under D1 is (−£1,500). This, in fact, is the worst decision that could have been made when D1 occurs. The decision maker considers what the best possible choice would have been. In this case it is option D with an NPV of (−£100). Thus the decision maker will regret having chosen A and the level of regret will be the difference between the NPV for the optimal choice under level of demand D1 and that for the option chosen:

Regret of having chosen A when D1 occurs = −£100 − (−£1,500) = £1,400.

Similarly, other regret values can be calculated. For example:

Regret of having chosen A when D2 occurs = +£225 − (−£250) = £475.
Regret of having chosen A when D3 occurs = −£175 − (−£575) = £400.
Regret of having chosen A when D4 occurs = +£2,350 − (+£2,350) = £0.
Regret of having chosen A when D5 occurs = +£770 − (+£770) = £0.

In the case where A is chosen and either D4 or D5 occurs, the decision maker will feel no regret, since option A is the optimal choice under these levels of demand. This process of calculating regret values is then undertaken for each of the other options and a regret table constructed as in Table 6.3.

Having constructed the regret table we now identify the maximum regret associated with each option:

Maximum regret for option A: £1,400.
Maximum regret for option B: £800.
Maximum regret for option C: £1,400.
Maximum regret for option D: £1,850.

Ms Noone now chooses the minimum of these maximums, namely *option B*. This is the option under which she will feel the least maximum regret if it turns out to be a sub-optimal decision.

While the minimax regret criterion can be considered to be more elaborate and sophisticated than some of the other approaches considered, nonetheless it does have its shortcomings. In particular, by only focusing on one value for each option, namely the maximum regret, it ignores a considerable amount of the information available to the decision maker. In spite of this weakness, the minimax regret approach does provide the decision maker with an alternative means by which to consider the investment decision and focuses attention on the opportunity cost of a sub-optimal decision.

Summary of game-theoretic approaches

The game-theoretic approaches provide the decision maker with additional means by which to consider the investment decision and thus give the person

Table 6.3 Values of regret for each option under different levels of demand

Demand Option	D1	D2	D3	D4	D5
A	£1,400	£475	£400	£0	£0
B	£650	£0	£800	£350	£270
C	£135	£225	£0	£1,400	£370
D	£0	£125	£25	£1,850	£470

Investment Decision Making under Conditions of Uncertainty: More Advanced Solutions

making the decision important information and insight. However, as mentioned previously, these approaches do not offer definitive advice. In the example used to illustrate the game-theoretic approaches the different criteria have not provided a consistent answer. This is exactly as to be expected, given that they emphasize different aspects of the options. For example, maximax is emphasizing the upside potential of the options, while maximin is concentrating on the downside risk.

Nonetheless, while consistent answers are not provided (and indeed are unlikely to be in many practical situations) one or more of the different approaches can be chosen to be used by the decision maker to reflect her risk preferences and attitudes. Most importantly, perhaps, the use of one of the five approaches outlined above is likely to improve the decision maker's understanding of the options available.

SUMMARY AND KEY POINTS

Following on from the discussion in the previous chapter of risk and uncertainty and some simple means for dealing with the related problems, this chapter has considered more advanced solutions to the problems caused when the outcome of an investment decision is not known with certainty. While decision tree analysis, simulation models and game-theoretic approaches provide more advanced means of considering these problems, they do not provide definitive answers. The decision maker is still required to make a decision. However, the techniques considered in this chapter do provide the decision maker with greater insight and their use should lead to the person taking the decision having a greater understanding of the projects being considered and the possible outcomes associated with those projects. The key points from this chapter are as follows:

- While the methods discussed in this chapter are less simplistic than those previously considered, it still needs to be remembered that the use of these techniques will not provide hard-and-fast decision rules.
- Decision tree analysis builds on the basic concept considered when discussing the ENPV approach in the previous chapter, where we saw that investment appraisal decisions would not be based on a single set of cash-flow estimates, relating to one set of assumptions.
- However, the decision tree approach refines the ENPV approach to take account of the dynamic nature of the environment in which firms operate.
- It provides decision makers with considerably more information about the possible payoffs from an investment opportunity than does the simple ENPV approach.
- In discussing sensitivity analysis we saw that it suffers from the shortcoming that it only gives consideration to movements in one variable at a time. Simulation techniques avoid this shortcoming by allowing the evaluation of changes in several variables simultaneously.

- A simulation model is a means by which a mathematical model is used to simulate the possible outcomes of a financial decision.
- With simulation techniques it is necessary to identify a probability distribution for the outcome for each variable.
- The use of a simulation technique requires a computer model to select an outcome for each variable at random from the probability distribution for each variable. On the basis of these selections a figure for NPV is calculated. The model is run a large number of times and a probability distribution for the NPV of the project can be determined.
- The approach has the advantage that it explicitly recognizes the interrelationships which exist between the different variables and provides the decision maker with much greater understanding of the factors which affect the cash flows of the project.
- The main disadvantage of the simulation approach is that it can be very time-consuming and very costly to gather the necessary information and to input the data into the simulation model.
- The decision maker needs to consider the costs of implementing a simulation model, the necessity for good-quality information to be input into the model and whether it is worthwhile incurring such costs.
- Game-theoretic approaches to investment decision making are concerned with situations where the decision maker has no knowledge of the probabilities of each possible outcome.
- The game-theoretic approaches provide the decision maker with means by which to consider the options available. They do not provide the decision maker with definitive advice, but do provide important information and insights.
- It is quite possible, indeed likely, that the five criteria will give conflicting advice since they emphasize different aspects of the options.
- All of the approaches considered in this chapter provide the decision maker with information regarding the projects under consideration and should improve the understanding of the factors which influence the profitability of each potential investment opportunity.

WORKED EXAMPLE

Trackstar plc, a sportswear company, is considering launching a new running shoe and must decide whether to aim for a mass market, whether to try to attract the middle range market of regular runners, or whether to aim the product specifically at serious athletes. These options are A, B and C. The company believes that the success of the new shoe will depend largely on the reactions of its competitors. Competitors will (1) not react, (2) launch a new advertising campaign for their existing products, or (3) launch a new running shoe which is directly in competition with the new product of Trackstar. Trackstar undertakes investment appraisal analysis and calculates the NPV of each option under each different scenario. The figures are as shown in the table.

| Competitor reaction | 1 | 2 | 3 |
Option	NPV (£000)	NPV (£000)	NPV (£000)
A	430	100	−440
B	390	200	−260
C	200	150	100

Show which option would be preferred when using:

(a) the Bayes–Laplace criterion;
(b) the maximax criterion;
(c) the maximin criterion;
(d) the Hurwicz criterion;
(e) the minimax regret approach.

In using the Hurwicz criterion show answers when using probability figures of 0.75 for the best outcome and 0.25 for the worst outcome and also when using probability figures of 0.25 for the best outcome and 0.75 for the worst outcome.

Answers:

(a) Assigning equal probabilities to each possible outcome allows us to calculate an ENPV figure for each option:

$$NPV_A = (430/3) + (100/3) - (440/3) = 30,$$
$$NPV_B = (390/3) + (200/3) - (260/3) = 110,$$
$$NPV_C = (200/3) + (150/3) + (100/3) = 150.$$

Using the Bayes–Laplace criterion, option C would be chosen.

(b) The maximum outcome for each option is as follows:

A: 430,
B: 390,
C: 200.

Therefore the maximax approach would choose option A.

(c) The minimum outcome for each option is as follows:

A: −440,
B: −260,
C: 100.

Therefore, the maximin approach would select option C.

(d) Using the Hurwicz criterion with weights of 0.75 for the best outcome and 0.25 for the worst outcome we obtain weighted payoffs as follows:

A: [0.75 × 430 + 0.25 × (−440)] = 212.5,
B: [0.75 × 390 + 0.25 × (−260)] = 227.5,
C: [0.75 × 200 + 0.25 × (100)] = 175.

Using these weights, the Hurwicz criterion selects option B. Now, using the Hurwicz criterion with weights of 0.25 for the best outcome and 0.75 for the worst outcome we obtain weighted payoffs as follows:

A: [0.25 × 430 + 0.75 × (−440)] = −222.5,
B: [0.25 × 390 + 0.75 × (−260)] = −97.5,
C: [0.25 × 200 + 0.75 × 100] = 125.

Using these weights, the Hurwicz criterion selects option C.

(e) With the minimax regret approach it is necessary to construct a regret table. If option A is chosen and competitors follow action (1), then the decision maker at Trackstar will feel no regret, since option A is the best outcome under scenario 1. However, if the competitor follows scenario 2, the decision maker will regret not having chosen option B and the level of regret will be (200 − 100) = 100. Similarly, if option A is chosen and scenario 3 results, then regret of (100 − (−440)) = 540 will be felt. Following a similar approach for when options B and C are chosen we can construct the regret table.

| Competitor reaction | 1 | 2 | 3 |
Option	Regret (£000)	Regret (£000)	Regret (£000)
A	0	100	540
B	40	0	360
C	230	50	0

The maximum regret associated with each option is:

Maximum regret for option A: £540.
Maximum regret for option B: £360.
Maximum regret for option C: £230.

Using the minimax regret criterion option C would be chosen.

QUESTIONS

6.1 In what ways is decision tree analysis superior to the ENPV approach? What are the main problems in implementing a decision tree analysis?

6.2 How, and in what circumstances, is a simulation model better for analysing an investment opportunity than is sensitivity analysis? Why is such an approach not always more desirable than simple sensitivity analysis?

6.3 Why do the five game-theoretic approaches to investment appraisal not provide consistent advice? Is this a problem?

6.4 The Bayes–Laplace criterion and the Hurwicz criterion both use probabilities to determine a money value associated with each project. How do the two approaches differ?

6.5 What is the basis of the minimax regret approach?

7 INVESTMENT APPRAISAL AND THE CAPITAL-ASSET PRICING MODEL

Introduction

We have now established very clearly that risk and uncertainty are pervasive problems when appraising investment opportunities. In the previous two chapters consideration has been given to *ad hoc* means by which decision makers can take account of these problems. However, as we stated in Chapter 5, while these *ad hoc* techniques provide useful practical guidelines for decision makers, their use introduces some subjectivity into the decision-making process. For this reason we need to consider a more formal, objective approach to dealing with these problems. In this chapter we give consideration to just such an approach, by discussing the capital-asset pricing model (CAPM). The CAPM represents one of the great strides forward in financial decision making in the post-Second World War period. Although it has been developed on the basis of rigorous academic theory, it has proved to be of considerable practical significance and financial decision makers make use of the implications of CAPM on a frequent basis. In discussing the CAPM in this chapter we will not concentrate on the formal derivation of the theory, but rather try to give an intuitive guide to the model and to how the model can assist decision makers faced with appraising investment opportunities characterized by uncertainty. In addition, the principles which underlie the CAPM will be explained. An understanding of these principles will be of considerable benefit to any decision maker who intends to make use of the CAPM when appraising investment opportunities characterized by uncertainty. Furthermore, knowledge of these principles will be of assistance to decision makers who are required to justify the use of the approach to their superiors.

It is worth stressing at this stage that the CAPM is a model which was developed with the specific purpose of valuing (or pricing) risky assets such as shares. However, the price of a share will in large part be determined by the riskiness of the returns from owning that share. In many ways, buying a share is similar to investing in a risky investment project: a certain outlay is undertaken at the time the share is purchased (i.e. there is the sacrifice of an immediate and certain level of consumption) and the purchaser will then receive dividends at different times in the future, although at the time of the purchase the level of future dividends is not known with certainty (i.e. the dividends represent an expected increase in future consumption). The fact that future dividends are uncertain, means that in pricing shares it will be necessary to discount future dividends to their present value, using a discount rate which takes into account the riskiness of the future dividend flow. This is directly analogous to discounting the future uncertain returns from an investment project to their present value to determine whether the project is worth undertaking. Thus, a model which is appropriate for pricing shares (and other risky capital assets) is also appropriate for helping to determine the discount rate to use when appraising a risky investment opportunity. The CAPM can, therefore, be considered as a means of objectively determining the risk premium to be added to the risk-free rate to arrive at an appropriate risk-adjusted discount rate. Before going on to consider the CAPM in detail, it is important to distinguish between different types of risk.

DISTINGUISHING BETWEEN TYPES OF RISK

When business risk was discussed in Chapter 5, it was implicitly assumed that while there are many sources of such risk, there is, nonetheless, only one *type* of business risk. In other words, it was implicitly assumed that 'risk is risk' and that in deriving a risk premium to use in any risk-adjusted discount rate approach it is not necessary to differentiate between types of (business) risk. However, as we shall see in this section, this approach to risk is simplistic and, more importantly, can lead to serious errors in deriving a risk-adjusted discount rate and, hence, to serious errors in decisions as to which investment projects to undertake. In particular, we shall see that rather than there being only one type of risk, there is a need to differentiate between two types of risk: systematic risk and unsystematic (or diversifiable) risk.

The concepts of systematic and unsystematic risk can be understood best by considering the various sources of risk which can affect an investment project. Generally speaking we can break these sources down into general sources of risk which affect all (or at least the vast majority of) firms in the economy, and firm-specific sources of risk which only affect certain companies. The general sources of risk include such things as the total level of consumer demand in the economy, the level of taxes, both direct and indirect, the level of interest rates, and the cost of energy. For example, if the economy is suffering from a recession (i.e. the level of consumer demand is low) then it is likely that *all* companies will be adversely affected and that sales revenues will fall for all companies. Similarly, a rise in taxes or a rise in interest rates or higher energy costs will impact adversely on *all* firms. The first two of these increases are likely to lead to lower sales revenue for all firms, while the last of the three could lead to a fall in consumer demand (since consumers will now be paying higher fuel bills) *and* to an increase in (energy) costs for firms. Thus, in the case of an increase in the cost of energy both revenues and costs may be affected.

Investment Appraisal and the Capital-Asset Pricing Model

While all companies may be affected by these general factors, it will clearly be the case that some companies are affected more adversely than are other companies. For example, when the economy is in recession bread manufacturers are likely to be affected less badly than are car manufacturers: in recession people still eat (and we can therefore say that bread manufacturers will continue to make dough!), but they are likely to postpone the purchase of new cars. Similarly, when the economy is booming, both bread manufacturers and car manufacturers are likely to benefit, but the latter will benefit more: there is only so much bread that people can eat (or only so much that they knead!), but more expensive cars may be purchased, or people may renew their cars more frequently. Thus the risk associated with these general factors will differ from firm to firm (and even from product to product within the same firm, since, for example, sales of luxury cars are likely to be affected more by the state of the economy than are sales of more basic cars) and it will be necessary to take account of the level of this type of risk when deciding upon the risk premium to add to determine the risk-adjusted discount rate. These general factors which affect all firms are the source of *systematic risk*.

In addition to the general factors which affect all firms, there are specific sources of risk which affect particular firms. Within the category of firm-specific risk are factors such as the effectiveness of a firm's advertising campaign, the success or otherwise of a firm's R&D policy, the state of industrial relations within the firm, and the ability and effectiveness of the management of the firm. These types of factors will be highly influential in determining the result of any investment project. For example, a highly profitable (in NPV terms) investment could very easily become a negative-NPV project if the firm undertaking the investment has a very ineffective advertising campaign, or if the firm is adversely affected by poor industrial relations leading to a prolonged strike by the workforce. However, an ineffective advertising campaign or a strike in one company does not impact on all firms. Rather, these firm-specific events impact on only one firm.[1] Specific factors are the sources of *unsystematic risk*.

From the firm's point of view it might appear that the distinction between general factors and specific factors is irrelevant. If anything happens which has an adverse impact on the firm's cash flow, it could be argued that it doesn't matter what the source of that impact is. However, from the point of view of the owners of the company the source of risk is important, and it is the point of view of the owners which should be taken into account when appraising investment opportunities.

WHY THE DISTINCTION BETWEEN SYSTEMATIC AND UNSYSTEMATIC RISK MATTERS

The reason why the distinction between the two types of risk is important from the owner's point of view is that one of the types of risk, unsystematic risk, can be avoided fairly easily and at little (almost zero) cost, while the other type, systematic, cannot be avoided if the owner is to remain owner. Let us consider how unsystematic risk can be avoided.

In discussing risk we normally think of the possibility of returns being worse than expected, in other words we typically consider downside risk. However, the positive aspect of risk is that there is the possibility that returns will be higher than expected, i.e. there is upside potential. Thus, in anticipating what returns will be in, say, the coming year, a decision maker will have some idea of the expected value of those returns. However, actual returns may turn out to be lower than expected or they may turn out to be higher than expected. For example, an unsuccessful advertising campaign may lead to lower than expected returns, while a highly successful advertising campaign may result in returns which are higher than expected.

As we have seen, unlike systematic risk, unsystematic risk affects only one firm at a time. However, the impact of unsystematic risk can either be good or bad, depending on, for example, whether the advertising campaign is successful or poor. An investor buying shares in a company does not know whether unsystematic risk will affect the firm in a positive or a negative way in the coming year. However, if the investor buys shares in a number of companies to create a portfolio of shares, then they can reasonably expect that while some companies will be adversely affected by poor advertising campaigns, other shares in the portfolio will be held in companies which benefit from successful advertising campaigns. Thus, by diversifying their ownership of shares, investors can avoid unsystematic risk. Another, more simplistic, example will help to illustrate further the benefits of diversification.

The returns from investing in an umbrella manufacturer are likely to be determined in part by the weather. In a year with a lot of rain the returns on shares in the umbrella manufacturer will go up (so too will umbrellas!). Similarly, in a year with little rain returns will fall. Thus, investors in an umbrella manufacturer face the risk associated with the weather. However, the returns from investing in an ice-cream producer will also be determined in part by the weather. When the weather is poor, ice-cream sales will fall and so will returns. In times of good weather, returns on shares in an ice-cream producer will rise. (On average, investors will get their just desserts!) Thus, by holding shares in both an umbrella manufacturer and an ice-cream producer, an investor can avoid the risk associated with the weather.

Similar arguments can be applied to all other sources of unsystematic risk: when one company is experiencing a period of unsuccessful R&D, another company will be proving successful in this area; when one firm is suffering from poor management, another will be benefiting from successful dynamic leadership; while one business is being adversely affected by poor labour relations, another will be going through a time of harmonious relations; and so on. The important point about this aspect of unsystematic risk is that an investor can avoid this type of risk altogether by holding a broadly diversified portfolio of shares. Thus, unsystematic risk can be avoided at almost zero cost (the only cost which the investor faces is the extra transactions costs from investing in shares in a number of companies, rather than in shares in only one business). Given that this risk can be avoided at almost zero cost, there will be no reason for companies to reward investors for this type of risk by paying out higher rates of return. Indeed, in a highly competitive market such as the London Stock Exchange, any company which did pay such a reward would find the demand for its shares rising, which would lead to a rise in the price of those shares and thus a fall in the rate of return. Thus, competitive pressures would ensure that investors are not rewarded for unsystematic risk.

In contrast to unsystematic risk, it is not possible to avoid the risk associated with general factors by holding shares in a large number of companies. When the economy is booming, *all* companies will benefit. Similarly, a rise in taxes will impact adversely on *all* businesses. Given that systematic risk cannot be avoided by diversification, investors can expect to receive an extra return for investing in shares of companies which are faced by more systematic risk. The higher the level of systematic risk, the higher should be the expected rate of return. Again, competitive pressures will ensure that this is the case. To illustrate, consider two companies which face the same level of systematic risk (they may, for example, be two car manufacturers) but which have shares which are priced such that the two companies offer different rates of return. For example, company A may be expected to pay annual dividends of 10p and have a share price of £2, while company B is also expected to pay annual dividends of 10p, but its shares are priced at only £1. In all other respects the two companies are identical. In such a situation, demand for shares in company B would rise, while demand for shares in company A would fall. These pressures of supply and demand will continue until the shares in the two companies are offering the same rate of return. Thus, companies with the same level of systematic risk will offer the same rate of return. Similarly, if two companies offer the same rate of return, but one has higher systematic risk, then risk-averse investors would demand shares in the company with less systematic risk, not demand shares in the company with more systematic risk, and prices would respond until the rate of return in the more risky (in systematic-risk terms) company is higher to reflect its level of systematic risk.

From the discussion in this section it can be seen that the distinction between systematic and unsystematic risk does matter. Investors will be rewarded for taking on systematic risk, but will not be rewarded for taking on unsystematic risk. Thus, in determining the appropriate rate of return from an investment it is not total risk which matters, but only systematic risk. Two companies may face the same level of total risk (as measured, say, by the standard deviation of returns), but offer different rates of return. However, two companies which face the same level of systematic risk must offer the same rate of return. Importantly, these rates of return are not plucked out of thin air, but rather are market-determined. Thus, there is an objective means by which rates of return are determined.

SYSTEMATIC RISK AND INVESTMENT APPRAISAL

This concept of market-determined rates of return can be applied to the appraisal of investment opportunities. The discount rate to be used in an investment appraisal calculation should reflect the riskiness of the project being considered. However, investors in a project can diverse away the unsystematic risk associated with the project by purchasing shares in a large number of companies. Therefore, it is only systematic risk which should be taken into account in deciding upon the risk premium to add to the risk-free rate to arrive at a riskadjusted discount rate. In Chapter 5 we argued that the risk-adjusted discount rate approach was a common-sense approach to the treatment of risk in investment appraisal. However, we also stated that the approach has the drawback of appearing to be objective, when, in fact, it is inherently subjective in that both the risk premium to be added and the classification of riskiness of a project required subjective decisions to be made. However, the CAPM appears to provide us with a market-determined (objective) means by which to measure risk and by which to measure the additional returns which a risky project should earn. It therefore appears to provide us with a means by which to arrive at a market-determined discount rate to use in the appraisal of investment opportunities. We must, however, examine how systematic risk and the return to systematic risk can be measured.

MEASURING SYSTEMATIC RISK AND THE REQUIRED RATE OF RETURN

In considering the measurement of systematic risk it is helpful to begin by considering the systematic risk of a company before going on to consider systematic risk at the individual-project level. As we have seen, systematic risk is that risk which is caused by general market-wide factors: factors which have an impact on the economy as a whole. Thus systematic risk is the risk which relates to systematic movements in the market. It, therefore, follows that in seeking to measure systematic risk we wish to have a measure of how returns from a particular company move in relation to movements in the returns in the economy as a whole. For example, a possible measure of how returns in the economy as a whole are moving is found by examining the returns on a very broad-based measure of returns activity, such as the FT All-Share Index. Changes in this index provide a measure of what is happening to returns on all shares listed on the London Stock Exchange. For example, the index rises from 2000 on the first day of January to 2100 on the first of February, then there has been a 5% increase in the index (the increase of 100 represents 5% of the starting value of the index of 2000) and the monthly returns on the market as a whole are 5%. If the index subsequently falls to 1953 on the first of March, this represents a fall of 7% (the fall of 147 is 7% of the starting value of 2100) and the monthly returns in this period are −7%.

The measure of the systematic risk of an individual company should measure how the returns on the shares in the individual company vary as the returns on the market vary. For example, if the share price of company A is £1.50 on the first of January, £1.65 on the first of February and £1.42 on the first of March, then the monthly returns on the share are 10% in the first month and (approximately) −14% in the second month. Thus, movements in the returns on shares in company A are twice those of the market: when the market goes up

5% the shares go up 10%, when the market goes down 7%, the shares fall by 14%. The measure of systematic risk should reflect the extent of the movement relative to the market.

A factor which is of central importance to the application of CAPM is the beta coefficient of an asset. The beta measures the risk of the company relative to the risk of the market as a whole. In the above example, the beta for company A (assuming the relationship identified for the period January to March continues over a longer period) is 2. Formally, the beta is measured as the ratio of the covariance of returns on the company and returns on the market to the variance of returns on the market. It can also be estimated by running a regression of returns on the individual shares against the returns on the market using historical data and using the slope coefficient as a measure of beta. (The meanings of these statistical terms can be found in any basic textbook on the subject.) Alternatively, there are business services which calculate and sell the value of beta for individual companies. Once the beta has been calculated (or obtained) the required rate of return is calculated as follows:

$$R_i = R_f + [R_m - R_f]\beta_i,$$

where R_i is the required rate of return (or discount rate), R_f is the risk-free rate of interest (for example, the rate on Government bonds), R_m is the return on the market as a whole (for example, the rate on the FT All-Share Index), and β_i is the company beta.

Thus, for example, if the risk-free rate of return is currently 6%, the return on the market as a whole averages 14% and the beta is 2 (as for company A above), then the required rate of return is

$$R_i = R_f + [R_m - R_f]\beta_i = 6 + [14 - 6]2 = 22\%.$$

This figure provides a measure of the required rate of return for the company as a whole. It will also provide an appropriate discount rate for individual projects, provided that any new project has the same level of systematic risk as the company as a whole. In many cases this will be appropriate. For example, a manufacturer of mass-market cars which is considering launching a new mass-market car may reasonably expect that the new project will have approximately the same systematic risk as the company as a whole. Thus the company beta can be used to calculate an appropriate discount rate for the project.

However, if the company is considering launching a new luxury car and this represents a departure from the normal line of business for the company, the company beta may well be inappropriate. In this case, the beta needs to be adjusted to reflect the fact that the new product will have greater systematic risk than the company as a whole. The company should then try to estimate the project beta rather than the company beta. Unfortunately this is not an easy thing to do. If the project is genuinely new then there may be no historic data on which to base estimates of the beta. It may then be necessary to estimate the beta by some other means. Often this requires the use of judgement; for example, the company may estimate that the beta for a luxury-car project should be 1.25 times that of the mass-market-car project beta. The problem with this is that subjectivity is again being introduced into the calculations. This represents one of the problems of applying the CAPM to actual project appraisal.

An alternative approach is for the company considering a project, say company Q, to estimate the beta for another company, say company Z. Company Z should be in exactly the same type of business as the project which company Q is considering. The beta for company Z could then be used as the beta for the project providing that the whole of the activities of company Z is in the line of business of the new project and that company Z and company Q have the same capital strucure. If the two companies have differing capital structures then an adjustment must be made to take account of the difference. This adjustment must be made because the asset beta will be a weighted average of the debt and equity betas. The beta on debt will almost always be less than the beta on equity in the same company, because there is less risk associated with the cash flows from owning debt compared to the cash flows from owning equity. Further difficulties can arise due to differences in taxation between the companies. The manner in which adjustments should be made for capital structure and taxation is beyond the scope of this book. Where adjustments are necessary it is advisable to seek professional advice as to how the adjustments should be made. However, the important point is that while such adjustments are difficult, they can be sensibly made. As a result, the CAPM remains valid in spite of its complexity.

DIFFICULTIES IN APPLYING CAPM

In addition to there being a problem of estimating betas for individual projects, the CAPM approach suffers from other problems when an attempt is made to operationalize the model. First, technically speaking the CAPM is a one-period model and the estimated required rate of return applies to one period only. Given that most projects are multi-period projects, there are problems in applying a model which is developed in a theoretical one-period world to practical projects. It is possible to extend the CAPM's use to a multi-period world, but application becomes very complex. Second, it is possible that betas are not stable through time. Thus, in one period a company may have an estimated beta of, say, 2, while in another period, the beta may be 1.8. While this difference is relatively small, using 1.8 rather than 2 in the estimate of the required rate of return calculated above, would lead to the discount rate falling from 22% to 20.4%. Such a difference could be sufficient to make the difference between a project's having a negative or a positive NPV. Third, as we have seen in the above discussion, estimation of the required rate of return is not easy. It either involves the use of considerable data (and possibly a computer) or the purchase of values from a business service. Thus, while the CAPM does represent a major stride forward in theory, the practical application of the model is quite complex and suffers from a number of shortcomings.

While there are undoubtedly problems associated with the application of the CAPM to practical project appraisal, nonetheless the CAPM does provide important insights for the decision maker. Of most significance is the fact that the CAPM clearly identifies the fact that it is not total risk which should be considered when attempting to determine a project discount rate. Rather, it is the extent to which returns on the project systematically vary with the returns on the market as a whole which is important. It is true that when a company undertakes a project it faces all of the risk associated with that project. However, the owners of the company can diversify their holdings in such a way that they can eliminate their exposure to the unsystematic risk of the project.

The actual use of the CAPM for determining a project discount rate is problematic and decision makers should be cautious in their use of the model. Nevertheless, by taking account of the major insight of the CAPM, decision makers should arrive at a more appropriate discount rate to use when making investment appraisal decisions. While subjectivity cannot be completely eliminated, the CAPM does provide a framework for obtaining a more objectively determined discount rate. In spite of this, it should be remembered that the use of the CAPM (or indeed any other model) cannot guarantee the success of a project. As has been stated previously, techniques designed to aid the decision maker should be used in conjunction with experience and judgement and they should not replace the decision-making process.

SUMMARY AND KEY POINTS

In this chapter consideration has been given to the capital-asset pricing model. The CAPM is a model which provides an objective means by which to measure and price risk, in contrast to the *ad hoc* approaches for dealing with risk and uncertainty which have been seen in earlier chapters. Although the CAPM has been developed on the basis of rigorous academic theory, nonetheless the implications of the model can and do provide sound practical advice for decision makers. Indeed, the main finding of the model is widely applied in practice in financial markets. The main implication of CAPM is that there are two types of risk, diversifiable and non-diversifiable and that only the latter is priced by financial markets. It is non-diversifiable, or systematic, risk which should be taken into account when determining the appropriate discount rate for an investment project. However, while the CAPM does provide sound practical advice, we have seen that there are problems associated with the use of the CAPM and that these need to be taken into account by decision makers seeking to use this model in investment appraisal. For this reason, the model needs to be used with caution.

The key points in this chapter are as follows:

- *Ad hoc* techniques of investment appraisal provide useful practical guidelines for decision makers. However, their use introduces some subjectivity into the decision-making process. For this reason a more formal, objective approach to dealing with these problems needs to be considered.

- The CAPM provides one approach for deriving an objective means for dealing with risk and as such represents one of the great strides forward in financial decision making in the post-Second World War period.

- An understanding of the principles which underlie the CAPM will be of benefit to decision makers who wish to use the CAPM and will enable them to justify the use of this approach when appraising investment opportunities.

- A model which is appropriate for pricing risky assets is also appropriate for helping to determine the discount rate to use when appraising a risky investment opportunity because there are strong similarities between buying a share and investing in a project. Both involve the forgoing of current consumption in return for the expectation of higher future consumption.

- Rather than there being only one type of risk, there is a need to differentiate between two types of risk: systematic risk and unsystematic risk.

- General sources of risk, including such things as the total level of consumer demand in the economy, the level of taxes, both direct and indirect, and the level of interest rates, affect all firms and are the source of *systematic risk*.

- There are also specific sources of risk which affect particular firms. For example, factors such as the effectiveness of a firm's advertising campaign, the success or otherwise of a firm's R&D policy, the state of industrial relations within the firm and the ability and effectiveness of the management of the firm are specific to the firm in question. These types of factor are the source of *unsystematic risk*.

- From the point of view of the owners of the company the source of risk is important because unsystematic risk can be avoided fairly easily and at little cost, while systematic risk cannot be avoided.

- An investor can avoid unsystematic risk altogether by holding a broadly diversified portfolio of shares. Thus, unsystematic risk can be avoided at almost zero cost. Thus, there is no reason for companies to reward investors for this type of risk by paying out higher rates of return.

- In contrast, it is not possible to avoid the risk associated with general factors by holding shares in a large number of companies. Since systematic risk cannot be avoided by diversification, investors can expect to receive an extra return for investing in shares of companies which are faced by more systematic risk.

- Investors in a project can diverse away the unsystematic risk associated with any project by purchasing shares in a large number of companies and, therefore, it is only systematic risk which should be taken into account in deciding upon the risk premium to add to the risk-free rate to arrive at a risk-adjusted discount rate.

- The CAPM provides us with a market-determined (objective) means by which to measure systematic risk and by which to measure the additional returns which a risky project should earn.

- In seeking to measure systematic risk we wish to have a measure of how returns from a particular company or project move in relation to movements in the returns in the economy as a whole.
- The beta coefficient measures the risk of the company relative to the risk of the market as a whole. Formally, it is measured as the ratio of the covariance of returns on the company and returns on the market to the variance of returns on the market. The beta can also be estimated by running a regression of returns on the individual shares against the returns on the market using historical data and using the slope coefficient as a measure of beta. Alternatively, there are business services which calculate and sell the value of beta for individual companies.
- The company or project beta can be used to calculate an appropriate discount rate for the project using the CAPM equation.
- Unfortunately, where a project is genuinely new there may be no historic data on which to base estimates of the beta. It may then be necessary to estimate the beta by some other means, which involves drawing on subjective views. Thus, the desired objectivity may be lost.
- Nonetheless, the CAPM does provide important insights for the decision maker. Of most significance is the fact that the CAPM clearly identifies the fact that it is not total risk which should be considered when attempting to determine a project discount rate.
- By taking account of the major insight of the CAPM, decision makers should arrive at a more appropriate discount rate to use when making investment appraisal decisions.
- However, the practical application of the model is quite complex and suffers from a number of shortcomings and it should be used with caution. In itself, the use of the CAPM cannot guarantee the success of a project. Techniques designed to aid the decision maker should be used in conjunction with experience and judgement and they should not replace the decision-making process.

QUESTIONS

7.1 Why is a model which was developed to explain the pricing of risky assets such as shares useful in the investment appraisal process?

7.2 Distinguish between systematic and unsystematic risk.

7.3 Which of the following are related to systematic risk and which to unsystematic risk:

(a) changes in direct tax rates;
(b) increases in the cost of copper;
(c) increases in the cost of oil;
(d) changes in the level of national income;
(e) changes in interest rates;
(f) the success or failure of advertising campaigns;
(g) the effectiveness of a management education programme within a company.

7.4 Why is the distinction between systematic and unsystematic risk important in the investment appraisal process given that a company faces both types of risk when undertaking an investment?

7.5 What do you understand by the term 'the beta coefficient'?

7.6 Specify the different types of information needed to calculate the discount rate when using the CAPM.

7.7 Explain why the company beta may not always be an appropriate figure to use when determining the discount rate for a particular project.

7.8 What is the major insight which the CAPM offers to decision makers considering investment opportunities?

NOTE

[1] Admittedly, a poor advertising campaign or a strike in one firm may have knock-on effects to other firms in the same industry. For example, the sales of firm A may benefit from the fact that its competitor, firm B, has an ineffective advertising campaign. However, the main impact of the event is on firm B and, importantly, not all firms in the economy are affected by the poor advertising campaign.

8 CAPITAL RATIONING

Introduction

In discussing the NPV rule in Chapter 4 we stated that 'under conditions of certainty the NPV method provides definite decision advice for independent projects: undertake those investment opportunities for which there is a positive NPV and do not undertake those investments for which the NPV is negative'. Having given attention to the problems caused by risk and uncertainty in the last three chapters, we now turn our attention to another problem which often arises in practice and which prevents the application of the simple instruction to undertake all positive NPV projects. The problem which we are going to consider in this chapter is the one caused by capital rationing. Attention will also be given to how decision makers must adjust the basic advice to undertake all positive-NPV projects when they are faced with capital rationing. To keep matters manageable we will again return to our assumption that decision makers have full knowledge regarding the outcomes of decisions which they take. The purpose of returning to this assumption is once again to gain understanding of the problems arising from, and the solutions to capital rationing. Clearly, in considering actual investment opportunities in the face of capital rationing, it is necessary to take into account the issues discussed in the last three chapters in relation to risk and uncertainty. However, for the purposes of this chapter these issues can be set to one side.

It is, perhaps, worth pointing out that all inputs to the investment process may be rationed. For example, there may be insufficient management expertise available to oversee all possible positive-NPV projects. Similarly, there may be a shortage of skilled labour or a shortage of raw materials which means that not all projects which add value to the firm can be undertaken. However, by far the most common form of rationing which firms face is in relation to the available capital. Indeed, as we shall see, the unavailability of, say, sufficient managerial expertise may lead to the firm 'imposing' capital rationing upon itself. The result of the problems which are caused by capital rationing is that the NPV method, which to this point has appeared almost invulnerable, can no longer be applied directly, even in a world of certainty.

As the name suggests, capital rationing relates to a situation in which companies are constrained in the amount of funds which they have available for investment purposes. As a result a firm has insufficient funds available to undertake all the positive-NPV projects which it would otherwise have the opportunity to pursue. One source of capital rationing arises from the fact that firms cannot always raise funds for investment from capital markets due to the imperfections of those markets. For example, capital markets may not be sufficiently confident about the firm's ability to make the project 'profitable', not because of any inherent problem with either the firm or the project, but because the market does not have sufficient information about the firm and the nature of the investment. A lack of information is a particular problem faced by small and new firms. Banks may be unwilling to lend funds for what is a perfectly reasonable investment opportunity because they simply do not know the details of those who are planning the investment: perhaps because the firm does not have a track record. Similar problems in raising funds can arise because of the costs of acquiring those funds: there can be very substantial transactions costs associated with obtaining money for investment.

While capital market imperfections are one source of capital rationing, it is more common for the firm to face a capital rationing situation because the firm itself chooses to limit the amount of investment which it will undertake. Thus, the firm decides that it will not undertake all positive-NPV projects. There are a number of major reasons why a firm may impose capital rationing upon itself. First, the firm may be unwilling to take on more debt because it believes that the lender will place unreasonable conditions on the firm. For example, lenders may place constraints on further borrowing or on the disposal of major assets during the life of the debt. Similarly, equity holders may be unwilling to issue more share capital because they do not wish to dilute their control of the firm. Again, this can be particularly true for new and small firms. However, a more common reason for self-imposed capital rationing is that management believes that there is an optimal growth profile for the firm and that if it expands too rapidly the firm will suffer as a result. For example, managers may believe that undertaking too many new projects at once will be unwieldy and will lead to a loss of control which has adverse consequences for the long-term viability of the firm. Thus, the firm chooses to impose a capital budget upon itself because of, for example, a lack of managerial or administrative expertise. Hence, it can be seen that the rationing of other inputs into the investment process can lead firms to ration the capital they have available for investment.

Capital rationing which is the result of money not being available from capital markets is typically referred to as 'hard rationing', while self-imposed capital rationing is known as 'soft rationing'. Whether capital rationing is the result of hard or soft rationing, it leads to a situation in which a choice has to be made between positive-NPV projects. The choice cannot simply be made by ranking the projects in terms of NPV, since the NPV does not give direct information about the amount of capital required to generate the NPV figure. Instead, it is necessary to give consideration not only to the NPV figure associated with a project, but also to the capital requirements of each project. In order to address the problems raised by capital rationing we need to distinguish between single-period capital rationing and multi-period capital rationing. Solutions to the problems differ depending upon the time horizon of the rationing.

SINGLE-PERIOD CAPITAL RATIONING

The most simple case of capital rationing arises when funds are limited for one period only, typically the current period. While the basic NPV rule can no longer be applied directly, there is a fairly straightforward means by which to deal with this problem. The means by which the problems caused by single-period capital rationing can be dealt with are best explained by considering an example. Imagine a situation in which a company has seven independent projects, projects A–G, which it is considering. The key features of these projects are shown in Table 8.1.

Using the standard NPV rule, and in the absence of capital constraints, six of the projects would be undertaken, since all but project E provide a positive NPV. However, the firm faces a capital constraint in year 0 of £720,000. Thus it is not able to undertake all positive-NPV projects (the six positive-NPV projects would require a capital outlay of £1.53m). However, we can begin by applying the basic rule that the company should not undertake negative-NPV projects: thus project E can be ruled out immediately. The question remains, how should the firm choose which of the six projects to undertake? Given that the aim is to maximize firm value, one way forward would appear to be to rank the projects by their NPV. On this basis G is the most preferred and D is the least preferred. Unfortunately, this does not provide us with much information, since the NPV figure alone does not provide information about the funds required for the project. Faced with a capital constraint of £720,000, the firm is not able to undertake the two projects yielding the highest NPV figures, G and A, since these projects combined require an outlay of £730,000.

The aim of the firm is to choose the combination of projects so as to

Table 8.1

Project	Outlay (£) in year 0	NPV	Rank by NPV
A	330,000	+100,000	2
B	270,000	+90,000	4
C	300,000	+95,000	3
D	80,000	+20,000	6
E	200,000	−50,000	7
F	150,000	+40,000	5
G	400,000	+180,000	1

maximize the NPV generated by using the available capital. We should therefore give consideration not to total NPV for each project, but to the NPV per pound of capital outlay required. Such a measure is provided by the benefit–cost ratio which can be expressed as follows:

Benefit–cost ratio = NPV/Capital outlay.

The benefit–cost ratio for each of the six projects is shown in Table 8.2, along with the ranking of each project on the basis of this ratio.

The benefit–cost ratio can now be used to rank the projects and to determine which projects to undertake, provided that the projects are divisible. By the term 'divisible' we mean that it is possible to undertake part of the project. Thus, for example, if the project is divisible it would be possible to undertake one-third of project A at a cost of £110,000 and generating an NPV of £33,333. If the projects are indeed divisible then the benefit–cost ratio approach can identify which of the above six projects to pursue. Projects G (ranked 1) and B (ranked 2) can be undertaken in their entirety, costing a total of £670,000. This leaves £50,000 of the £720,000 capital available. This £50,000 can then be devoted to the third ranked project: project C. However, project C costs £300,000. Therefore only one-sixth of project C can be undertaken. By pursuing projects G, B and one-sixth of C the total NPV will be £285,833.

In practice projects are very often not divisible in the way described above. In such a situation the benefit–cost ratio cannot provide the decision maker with the advice he or she needs. Rather, the decision maker must consider all possible combinations of the six projects which require capital of £720,000 or less and choose that combination which yields the highest total NPV. Possible combinations and the total NPVs for each are shown in Table 8.3.

From this table it can be seen that projects C and G should be undertaken, yielding a total NPV of £275,000 and using capital of £700,000. The remaining £20,000 can be ignored for the purposes of the calculations. While it would be possible to earn a return on this money by, say, depositing it in an interest-bearing account, the earnings should then be discounted at the appropriate discount rate, which should be the interest rate earned, since this reflects the market's view of the riskiness of the project. Thus the NPV on this 'project' (i.e. the investment of the extra £20,000) is zero.

In the example which we have just considered, the capital rationing relates to

Table 8.2

Project	Outlay (£) in year 0	NPV	Benefit–cost (B–C) ratio	Rank by B–C ratio
A	330,000	+100,000	0.303	4
B	270,000	+90,000	0.333	2
C	300,000	+95,000	0.316	3
D	80,000	+20,000	0.250	6
F	150,000	+40,000	0.267	5
G	400,000	+180,000	0.450	1

Table 8.3

Combination of projects	Total NPV
A + B + D	£210,000
A + C + D	£215,000
A + D + F	£160,000
B + C + D	£205,000
B + C + F	£225,000
B + G	£270,000
C + D + F	£155,000
C + G	£275,000
D + F + G	£240,000

year 0. Another possibility for single-period rationing is that there is no capital rationing in the current year, but that there is rationing in a future year. Consider, for example, a situation where capital is rationed in year 1, with there being only £400,000 available at that time. Again let us consider the six projects referred to earlier, but this time we must also consider their capital requirements in year 1 (see Table 8.4).

Given that projects B and F require no capital outlay in year 1 they can be pursued without giving consideration to their capital requirements. However, the remaining four projects must be ranked in terms of their year-1 benefit–cost ratio (which we will call BC1). The BC1 is calculated as the NPV divided by the outlay in year 1. For the four remaining projects BC1 is as follows:

$$\begin{aligned}
\text{A} \quad & 100/175 = 0.571, \\
\text{C} \quad & 95/150 = 0.633, \\
\text{D} \quad & 20/100 = 0.200, \\
\text{G} \quad & 180/350 = 0.514.
\end{aligned}$$

The projects can then be ranked by the BC1: C, A, G, D. If the projects are divisible then, in addition to pursuing projects B and F, projects C and A can be undertaken in their entirety and 75/350 of project G can be undertaken. If the projects are not divisible then all possible combinations requiring outlay of £400,000 or less in year 1 must be considered (see Table 8.5). In this case projects A and C should be undertaken (again in addition to projects B and F).

Table 8.4

Project	Outlay (£) in year 0	Outlay (£) in year 1	NPV
A	330,000	175,000	+100,000
B	270,000	0	+90,000
C	300,000	150,000	+95,000
D	80,000	100,000	+20,000
F	150,000	0	+40,000
G	400,000	350,000	+180,000

Table 8.5

Combination of projects	Total NPV
A + C	£195,000
A + D	£120,000
C + D	£115,000
G	£180,000

In the discussion so far on single-period capital rationing, consideration has been given to independent projects. We now turn to the situation where some projects are mutually exclusive. Let us consider the case of year-0 capital rationing as first discussed in this section. However, let projects C and G be mutually exclusive. Again, we first consider the case where projects are divisible. With mutually exclusive projects it is necessary to rank projects by their B–C ratio, but first excluding one of the mutually exclusive projects and then excluding the other. Consider the five projects from the above six, excluding project G. On the basis of the benefit–cost ratio the projects are ranked: B, C, A, F, D. Projects B and C can be undertaken in their entirety (requiring £570,000 capital) and 150/330 of project A could be undertaken. This would yield a total NPV of £(90,000 + 95,000 + (150/330)100) = £230,455.

Next, consider the five projects from the above six, excluding project C. On the basis of the benefit–cost ratio the projects are ranked: G, B, A, F, D. Projects G and B can be undertaken in their entirety (requiring £670,000 capital) and 50/330 of project A could be undertaken. This would yield a total NPV of £(180,000 + 90,000 + (50/330)100) = £285,152. On this basis it is the latter set of projects which should be undertaken and, of the mutually exclusive projects, C should not be undertaken.

If the projects are not divisible, then again we need to consider all possible combinations costing £720,000 or less, but this time excluding combinations involving both C and G. From Table 8.3 we can see that the best combination of this type involves the undertaking of projects B and G with a total NPV of £270,000.

The above discussion demonstrates that in the presence of single period capital rationing it is relatively straightforward to determine which projects to undertake. However, in practice, capital rationing does not exist for one period only. It is therefore necessary to give consideration to the problems caused by multi-period capital rationing and to potential solutions to those problems.

MULTI-PERIOD CAPITAL RATIONING

In most situations where a firm is faced with a number of investment opportunities the firm is also faced by capital constraints which exist not for only one period, but for many periods. In situations where projects only require a net cash outflow in the first year, multi-period capital rationing is no different from single-period capital rationing, since capital is only required for one year. However, many investment projects require net outlays in each of a number of years. In such circumstances the capital outlay in each year must be considered in relation to capital constraints which exist for each year. Clearly, in trying to choose the combination of projects to undertake which maximizes NPV the company faces as many constraints as there are years in which capital is rationed.

In the case of multi-period capital rationing the benefit–cost ratio cannot be used as a means by which to rank and choose projects. Instead, it is necessary to recognize the very substantially increased complexity of the situation and use a mathematical approach to find a solution to the problem. Once again, the firm is faced with choosing the combination of projects which maximizes the total NPV. Thus, the firm faces an optimization problem. Mathematical techniques have been developed to solve optimization problems and many are available and readily accessible in fairly inexpensive computer packages. One such technique will be considered here: namely, linear programming. While the suggestion of using a mathematical solution and reference to linear programming may appear to be complex to some decision makers, the principle and the use of the technique are fairly easily understood. Linear programming involves the decision maker in specifying an objective function (which in this case means specifying the details of how NPV would be maximized) and specifying the constraints which the decision maker faces. An example will help to illustrate the use of linear programming.

We will begin by considering a firm which is faced by six independent projects, H–M. For the time being the assumption will be made that the projects are divisible and have constant returns to scale (i.e. if the firm undertakes, for example, 0.3 of the project the NPV of the 'part-project' will be 0.3 of the NPV of the whole project). The firm faced with the six projects faces capital constraints in each of five years. In the present time (year 0) the maximum available capital is £800,000. In each of the following four years (years 1–4) only £200,000 capital is available. The key features of the six projects are shown in Table 8.6.

It can be seen from the table that while some projects do not require cash outflows in each of the five years (for example, K only requires a net cash outflow in year 0), some do, and all except K require a net cash outlay in more

Table 8.6

Project	Cash flows (£000s)					NPV (£000s)
	Year 0	Year 1	Year 2	Year 3	Year 4	
H	−120	−80	−160	−140	−100	+85
I	−40	−100	−120	−120	−140	+160
J	−230	−90	+60	+80	+80	+100
K	−450	+70	+70	+70	+120	+220
L	−75	−40	−10	+45	+85	+20
M	−200	−100	−100	−40	−40	+80

The reinvestment of cash inflows allows all of project H to be undertaken (at the expense of some of project J), leading to an increase in NPV to £547,609. Note that, now, the only year in which the full capital available appears to be used is year 0. However, the net-capital-required figures relate to capital requirements *in excess of* cash inflows. Thus, for example, in year 1 capital requirements are £80,000 for project H, £100,000 for project I, £74,340 for project J (equal to 0.826 times £90,000), and zero for project K. Total capital requirements in year 1 are, therefore, £254,340. However, £70,000 of this amount comes from project K, leaving a net capital required of £184,340. Hence, we can see that the use of cash inflows to ease capital constraints can have a significant impact on total NPV. Nonetheless, it should be noted that in practice many firms will not want to rely on future projected cash inflows to ease capital constraints, because the cash inflows are not guaranteed. For example, if the cash inflow from project K expected in year 1 were delayed the firm would not be able to provide all of the capital required for the other projects which it had commenced and a choice would have to be made about which project not to fund. Clearly, having already committed large sums to each of the projects this would be highly undesirable and have severe consequences for total NPV. Given that cash inflows are uncertain, it may be wise to act on the basis that such inflows are not available for reinvestment.

Up to now we have assumed that projects are divisible and offer constant returns to scale. In practice, many projects are not divisible. In such circumstances linear programming does not provide the complete answer. However, there is an alternative to linear programming which can be used in cases where projects are not divisible (i.e. are all-or-nothing projects); this is integer programming. Integer programming is very similar to linear programming, but now the additional constraint is imposed that the proportions h, i, j, k, l and m must be integers (i.e. must be whole numbers). Given the constraints we have already imposed on these proportions, this means that each must be either zero or one. Again, many packages are available to carry out integer programming. Indeed, the software which was used to calculate the answers above, has the ability to undertake integer programming, by simply specifying that the six proportions be integers. The optimum mix of projects is this case and the other details are shown below for the case where no reinvestment of interim cash flows is possible:

Proportion invested in each project:	Capital required each year (£000):
$h = 0$	Year 0: 720
$i = 1$	Year 1: 190
$j = 1$	Year 2: 120
$k = 1$	Year 3: 120
$l = 0$	Year 4: 140
$m = 0$	

NPV = £480,000

In this case the solution is very similar to that of the original example, except that now none of project H is undertaken, in no year is the full amount of capital available used, and the NPV has fallen by over £10,000.

If we now allow reinvestment of interim cash inflows the integer solution is as follows:

Proportion invested in each project:	Net capital required each year (£000):
h = 0	Year 0: 795
i = 1	Year 1: 160
j = 1	Year 2: 0
k = 1	Year 3: −75
l = 1	Year 4: −145
m = 0	

NPV = £500,000

Reinvestment now allows an additional project to be undertaken (project L) and leads to a situation in which in years 3 and 4 the net capital required is negative (i.e. cash inflows exceed capital outflows). As a result of the possibility of reinvestment the NPV has risen by £20,000 to £500,000. However, the potential problems of relying on interim cash inflows, which were mentioned earlier, again need to be borne in mind.

While we need to remember that there are problems associated with reinvestment of cash inflows and project divisibility, nonetheless, linear programming and integer programming provide valuable and relatively easy-to-implement means by which to consider the problems raised by multi-period capital rationing. Once again, the important point to bear in mind is that there are means by which to tackle the problems and that by setting out the objective and the constraints the decision maker is more likely to reach a decision which maximizes the value of the firm.

SUMMARY AND KEY POINTS

We have seen in this chapter that the simple advice to undertake all positive-NPV projects cannot typically be applied due to firms' facing problems associated with capital rationing. Furthermore, we have seen that capital constraints are often self-imposed in that firms place limits on the amount of capital they will commit to investment to avoid problems such as too rapid expansion. Given that the standard NPV rule can no longer be simply applied, we have considered other means for aiding the decision maker. The benefit–cost ratio was discussed in relation to single-period capital rationing and was shown to be a useful tool. However, when we turned to the more typical situation of multi-period capital rationing we saw that it is necessary to consider programming solutions to the problem. Computer packages which undertake programming solutions are widely available and we have seen how to go about setting up linear and integer programming problems by specifying the objective function and the constraints faced. The key points in this chapter are as follows:

- All inputs to the investment process may be rationed. However, by far the most common form of rationing which firms face is in relation to the available capital.

- Capital rationing relates to a situation in which companies are constrained in the amount of funds which they have available for investment purposes. As a result a firm has insufficient funds available to undertake all the positive-NPV projects which it would otherwise have the opportunity to pursue.
- Capital rationing that is the result of money not being available from capital markets is typically referred to as 'hard rationing', while self-imposed capital rationing is known as 'soft rationing'.
- When faced with capital rationing the aim of the firm is to choose the combination of projects so as to maximize the NPV generated by using the available capital.
- In the case of single-period capital rationing where projects are divisible we should give consideration not to total NPV for each project, but to the NPV per pound of capital outlay required. Such a measure is provided by the benefit–cost ratio.
- In practice, projects are very often not divisible and the benefit–cost ratio cannot provide the decision maker with the advice which he or she needs. Rather, the decision maker must consider all possible combinations of the positive-NPV projects which can be undertaken with the capital available.
- In the presence of single-period capital rationing it is relatively straightforward to determine which projects to undertake. However, in practice, capital rationing does not exist for one period only and it is necessary to give consideration to the problems caused by multi-period capital rationing.
- Many investment projects require net outlays in each of a number of years and the capital outlay in each year must be considered in relation to capital constraints which exist for each year.
- In trying to choose the combination of projects to undertake which maximizes NPV the company faces as many constraints as there are years in which capital is rationed.
- In the case of multi-period capital rationing it is necessary to recognize the very substantially increased complexity of the situation and use a mathematical approach to find a solution to the problem.
- Mathematical techniques have been developed to solve optimization problems and many are available and readily accessible in fairly inexpensive computer packages.
- Linear programming and integer programming involve the decision maker in specifying an objective function (which in this case means specifying the details of how NPV would be maximized) and specifying the constraints which the decision maker faces.
- Linear programming is suitable where projects are divisible and offer constant returns to scale, whereas integer programming should be used where the projects are of an 'all-or-nothing' variety.
- In specifying the constraints for the programming solution the decision maker needs to consider whether interim cash inflows can be used for reinvestment (i.e. to help meet capital requirements). While the use of interim cash inflows can ease capital constraints and greatly increase total NPV, their projected use needs to be given considerable thought as they are by no means certain.

- Given that cash inflows are uncertain, it may be wise to act on the basis that such inflows are not available for reinvestment.
- While capital rationing does present the decision maker with problems, those problems are surmountable and there are many readily available and easily accessible packages to assist the decision maker.

WORKED EXAMPLES

8.1 *Single-period capital rationing*

A company is considering a number of independent investment opportunities, the main financial details of which are shown in the table.

Project	Outlay (£) in year 0	NPV
A1	100,000	+40,000
A2	140,000	+45,000
A3	210,000	+65,000
A4	230,000	+75,000
A5	90,000	+30,000

The company faces a capital constraint in year 0 and can only invest £300,000 in that year, in spite of all five projects being desirable in NPV terms.

Required:

(a) Rank the projects by their NPV.

(b) Calculate the benefit–cost ratio for each project and rank the projects on the basis of the ratio.

(c) Which projects should be undertaken if the projects are divisible and what will be the total NPV?

(d) Which projects should be undertaken if the projects are not divisible and what will be the total NPV?

Answers:

(a) On the basis of the NPV the projects would have the following ranking:

A1: 4,
A2: 3,
A3: 2,
A4: 1,
A5: 5.

(b) The benefit–cost ratio is calculated by dividing the NPV by the initial capital outlay. The ratio for each project and the ranking on this ratio are as in the table.

Worked Examples

LIVERPOOL
JOHN MOORES UNIVERSITY
AVRIL ROBARTS LRC
TEL. 0151 231 4022

117

Project	B–C ratio	Ranking
A1	0.4	1
A2	0.321	4
A3	0.310	5
A4	0.326	3
A5	0.333	2

(c) If the projects are divisible, then projects should be undertaken on the basis of the ranking of the B–C ratio until all of the £300,000 has been utilized. Thus, all of project A1 and all of project A5 should be undertaken. This would require a capital outlay of £190,000. The third ranked project is A4, which requires more capital than is available once A1 and A5 have been undertaken. Thus, it is not possible to undertake all of project A4. Given that £110,000 of the capital remains available (£300,000 − £190,000), then the proportion 110/230 of project A4 should be undertaken, yielding an NPV from A4 of (110/230) × £75,000 = £35,870. Thus the total NPV = £40,000 + £30,000 + £35,870 = £105,870.

(d) If the projects are not divisible, then it is necessary to consider all possible combinations of the five projects which can be undertaken within the capital constraint of £300,000:

Combination of projects	Total NPV
A1 + A2	£85,000
A1 + A5	£70,000
A3 + A5	£95,000
A4	£75,000

On this basis it is desirable to undertake projects A3 and A5 and the total NPV will be £95,000.

8.2 *Multi-period capital rationing*
A company is considering a number of independent investment opportunities, the main financial details of which are shown in the table.

Project	Year 0	Year 1	Year 2	Year 3	Year 4	NPV £000s
		Cash flows (£000s)				NPV
A6	−70	−40	+20	+40	+60	+40
A7	−90	−60	−40	−20	−70	+60
A8	−110	−50	−30	−30	−30	+60
A9	−300	−20	+10	+30	+50	+120
A10	−170	−70	−30	−30	−85	+90

The company faces capital constraints as follows:

Year 0:	£450,000,
Year 1:	£140,000,
Years 2–4:	£50,000.

You are required to set up the problem into a form suitable for solution by linear programming by assuming that the projects are divisible and by:

(a) specifying the objective function;

(b) specifying the capital constraints, assuming that net cash inflows cannot be reinvested;

(c) specifying any other constraints.

Answers:

Let the proportion of project A6 which is to be undertaken be represented by m. Similarly, let the proportions of A7–A10 which are to be undertaken be represented by n, p, q and r respectively.

(a) The objective function specifies how the NPV would be maximized and is as follows:

$$40,000m + 60,000n + 60,000p + 120,000q + 90,000r.$$

(b) The capital constraint in year 0 is as follows:

$$70,000m + 90,000n + 110,000p + 300,000q + 170,000r \leq 450,000.$$

Similarly, for years 1–4 the capital constraints are as follows:

Year 1: $40,000m + 60,000n + 50,000p + 20,000q + 70,000r \leq 140,000,$
Year 2: $40,000n + 30,000p + 30,000r \leq 50,000,$
Year 3: $20,000n + 30,000p + 30,000r \leq 50,000,$
Year 4: $70,000n + 30,000p + 85,000r \leq 50,000.$

(c) The only other constraints which are required are that the proportions m, n, p, q and r must all be greater than or equal to zero and less than or equal to one.

QUESTIONS

8.1 Outline the implications of capital rationing for the implementation of the basic NPV decision advice rule.

8.2 Distinguish between soft and hard capital rationing.

8.3 In what circumstances is the benefit–cost ratio of use?

8.4 What is the difference between linear programming and integer programming?

8.5 Why is it usually not sensible to take account of cash inflows as being available for reinvestment and as a means of easing capital constraints faced by the firm?

9 **THE COST OF CAPITAL**

Introduction

In this chapter we will take another look at the question of how to determine the value of the discount rate which is to be used when discounting cash flows to arrive at an NPV figure. In Chapter 7 we examined the capital asset pricing model (CAPM) and saw how this could be used to provide a value for the required rate of return from a risky investment, which could then be used as a discount rate. Here we will consider the issue of the discount rate from the point of view of the cost of capital. The rate of return and the cost of capital can be thought of as two sides of the same coin. To the company the payment which is made to the providers of funds represents a cost of capital. To the providers of funds it represents a rate of return. In considering the CAPM we saw that this approach gave consideration to the return which investors would expect, given the riskiness of the investment, where riskiness relates to the systematic or non-diversifiable risk of the investment. The cost of capital method for determining the discount rate approaches the same issue from a different angle: namely, it gives direct consideration to the cost of the funds which will be used for investment.

The two approaches to determining the appropriate discount rate start from very different positions, and make different implicit assumptions. In Chapter 7 we saw that while the CAPM provided an approach which had great merit in theory, in practice there are substantial problems in applying the implications of CAPM to specific investments. These problems make the use of a different approach desirable. However, as we shall see, the approach based on the cost of capital is not without its problems. In spite of these problems, the cost of capital approach to determining the discount rate is of considerable use and has great intuitive appeal, focusing as it does on the cost of funds used to finance the investment. Given that companies do not typically raise funds from only one source, it is necessary to determine the cost of all funds used and then to weight the costs of different sources of funds to arrive at an average-cost-of-capital figure. Such a figure is normally referred to as the 'weighted average cost of capital' (or the WACC). To gain an understanding of how to calculate the WACC, consideration needs to be given to the sources of funds. Given that it is long-term funds which are usually used for investments, it is these types of funds which we need to consider. Although there are also short- and medium-term funds available, such funds are not suitable for long-term investments. While the distinction between long-term funds and short- and medium-term funds is somewhat arbitrary, it is usual to refer to funds which have either no fixed repayment date or at least ten years until repayment is due as 'long-term funds'. The calculation of the WACC requires the decision maker to first identify all sources of long-term funds, then to calculate the cost of the individual sources of funds, before weighting the costs of the individual funds. The weight for each source of funds is based upon its proportion of the total funds.

SOURCES OF LONG-TERM FUNDS

There are essentially two sources of long-term finance for investment purposes: namely, equity capital and debt capital. While distinctions are made between different types of equity capital (for example, between ordinary shares and preference shares) and while there are many different types of debt which can be issued, all sources of funds falls into one or other of these two categories. (Some sources of funds can be considered to be a mixture of both debt and equity. For example, convertible loan stocks are debentures (debt capital) which grant the holder the option to convert the stock into ordinary shares (equity capital) at a specified price on or between specific dates. However, for the purposes of understanding the concept and calculation of the WACC it is sufficient to consider equity and debt capital separately.) Similarly, while long-term funds come both from within the firm (in the form of retained earnings) and from external sources, again all such forms of funding are either in the form of equity capital or debt capital. The ratio of debt to equity in the mix of capital in the firm is known as the 'gearing ratio' or simply the 'level of gearing'.

Equity capital

The holders of equity capital own the company. In large companies, equity capital is often referred to as 'share capital', or simply 'shares', since ownership is spread among many shareholders by issuing many shares, each share representing a share of ownership of the company as a whole. This share gives the holder a share of any profits which are earned by the company. Equity capital represents the risk capital of the company. Shares are purchased from the company when the shares are issued or from shareholders who are selling their shares. When the shares are first issued by the company, the company sells the shares through the primary market and receives the funds to use for the operation of the company. When shares are sold by one shareholder to a new shareholder, the claim to ownership transfers to the new owner and the company does not receive any funds from the sale. Such a sale takes place on the secondary market. While the shareholders own the company, shares do not involve any guarantee that the shareholders will receive a return on their investment or that the amount invested will be repaid. Since shareholders have a claim on the profits and assets of the company, they can expect to receive a high return when the company is particularly profitable, but at times of low profitability or of losses, the shareholders may receive no income from their investment. In the worst case, the company may go bankrupt and the shareholders may lose their entire investment. This is why share capital is known as 'risk capital'.

The holders of equity capital are said to have a 'residual claim' on the assets of the company. They own all profits once all creditors of the company have been paid. This will be good in times of high profits, since there is likely to be a large sum of money which belongs to the shareholders once all creditors have received the money to which they are entitled. However, in times of low or zero profit, having a residual claim may mean that no income is received. The creditors of the company include holders of debt capital. As a result of debt holders having a 'prior claim' on the assets of the company, equity capital is viewed as being more risky than debt capital. Thus, equity holders will have to be paid a higher average (or expected) rate of return than debt holders to encourage them to invest in the company.

In practice, the vast majority of equity funds used for investment within a company does not come in the form of new share issues, but rather in the form of retained earnings. However, those retained earnings are equity funds and should earn a rate of return in line with other equity funds. The reason for this is that when a company generates earnings over and above the money due to its creditors, that money belongs to the shareholders of the company. The company may either pay the money out to shareholders in the form of dividends, or may retain earnings for reinvestment. The company should only retain earnings for reinvestment if it faces positive-NPV investment opportunities. Such investment opportunities will generate higher earnings in the future which will lead to there being higher dividends in the future. This in turn will lead to the share price increasing.

We can see the reason for this by considering what it is that determines the price of a share. The price will depend on the return which the investor expects to get when buying the share. The return which shareholders receive can come in two forms. First, shareholders will be paid dividends in each year that they own the shares. Second, share prices will move up and down through time and, thus, shareholders will experience capital gains and losses through time. The reason why share prices move through time is that expectations about future dividends change. As we saw in Chapter 7, in many ways buying a share is similar to investing in an investment project: a certain outlay is undertaken at the time the share is purchased (i.e. there is the sacrifice of an immediate and certain level of consumption) and the purchaser will then (hope to) receive dividends at different times in the future. In a market which values shares on the basis of fundamentals, the price of a share will be determined by the flow of benefits which the owner of the share expects to receive during the time that the share is held. If an investor buys a share today, holds it for a year at which time he or she receives a dividend and then sells the share, the flow of benefits from ownership will be made up of the dividend to be received in a year's time plus the share price received when the share is sold in a year's time. Given that both elements of the benefit flow will not be received for a year, it is necessary to discount those benefits to their present value to determine the current value of the share, i.e. to determine the price of the share. Thus the share price is given by:

$$P_0 = \frac{D_1 + P_1}{(1 + k_e)} \qquad (9.1)$$

where P_0 is the current share price, D_1 is the dividend to be received in a year's time, P_1 is the share price in one year's time, and k_e is the rate of return required by equity holders for securities of this risk class. (To keep matters simple we will ignore the problems caused by uncertainty and assume that D_1 and P_1 are known with certainty. In practice, the level of risk will affect the value of k_e.)

However, the share price in one year's time will be determined by the benefits that the next owner expects to get from ownership. If the next owner also holds the share for a year, then he or she will receive dividends at the end of year 2 plus the share price at the end of year 2. Thus, the price he or she will be willing to pay at the end of year 1 will be:

$$P_1 = \frac{D_2 + P_2}{(1 + k_e)} \qquad (9.2)$$

where P_1 is the share price at year 1, D_2 is the dividend to be received in two years' time, and P_2 is the share price in two years' time. Substituting this into equation (9.1) gives:

$$P_0 = \frac{D_1}{(1 + k_e)} + \frac{D_2}{(1 + k_e)^2} + \frac{P_2}{(1 + k_e)^2} \,. \qquad (9.3)$$

Of course, the share price to be received at the end of year 2 will be determined by the flow of benefits the next shareholder expects to receive. By continuing this argument and continually substituting into equation (9.1) we can see that the current share price is the discounted flow of all future dividends for as long as the share pays dividends, i.e. for infinity:

$$P_0 = \frac{D_1}{(1 + k_e)} + \frac{D_2}{(1 + k_e)^2} + \frac{D_3}{(1 + k_e)^3} + \frac{D_4}{(1 + k_e)^4} + \frac{D_5}{(1 + k_e)^5} + \dots \qquad (9.4)$$

Thus,

$$P_0 = \sum_{t=1}^{\infty} \frac{D_t}{(1 + k_e)^t} \,. \qquad (9.5)$$

Equation (9.5) is the dividend share valuation model. It shows that the value of a firm's shares is determined by the future flow of dividends, discounted by the rate of return required by shareholders. If positive-NPV investments are undertaken using retained earnings, then current dividends will be lower. However, in present-value terms future dividends should rise by more than the fall in current dividends, which will lead to a rise in the share price. However, if retained earnings are used to fund negative-NPV investments then the rise in (the present value of) future dividends will not be sufficient to warrant the fall in current dividends, and thus the price will fall. Given that changes in the share price represent part of the return to the shareholder and that retaining earnings for investment will lead to a change in the share price, it can be seen that retained earnings represent equity investment. Thus, equity funding consists of both new issues and retained earnings. It is the riskiness of the investment which determines the required rate of return and this should be the same irrespective of which form of equity funding is used, i.e. irrespective of whether the funds come from retained earnings or a new share issue. This is a very important point to understand and it is vital that retained earnings are not somehow viewed as either 'free' funds (i.e. they are not funds which have no cost) or as being relatively risk-free because they are readily available. It is not the source of equity funds (i.e. retained earnings or new share issues) which determines the riskiness of equity capital, but rather the use to which those equity funds are put. In other words, it doesn't matter whether equity funds come from retained earnings or a new issue; riskiness, and hence the cost of equity capital, will be determined by the riskiness of the project being undertaken.

Debt capital

Debt capital is also known as 'loan stock', 'bonds' or 'debentures'. The holders of debt capital do not receive a share of ownership of the company when they provide funds to the firm. Rather, when debt capital is first issued by a company the providers of debt capital purchase a debenture which involves their *lending* money to the firm. In return for lending this money, debenture holders have a right to certain guaranteed payments during the life of the bond. For example, it might be the case that a company issues loan stock in units of £100 in 1997 which states that the holders of the loan stock will receive £8 per annum for the period of the loan and the principal of £100 will be repaid in fifteen years' time, i.e. in 2012. This loan stock requires the company to make annual payments of £8 to the holders of the stock for the next fifteen years and also to repay the £100 in the year 2012, irrespective of the level of profits or losses which the company makes during that period. Thus, even if the company makes a very substantial loss in, for example, the year 1999, it must still make the payment of £8 to each holder of loan stock. If it does not make these payments or if it does not repay the principal when it is due to be repaid, the debt holders can force the company into bankruptcy. It is this right to payments irrespective of the performance of the company which is the reason why debt holders are said to have a 'prior claim' on the assets of the company and this prior claim means that from the point of view of the providers of funds, debt capital is less risky than equity capital and therefore requires a lower rate of return. Thus the cost of debt capital is lower than the cost of equity capital.

In addition to the fact that debt capital is cheaper than equity capital because debt holders face less risk, debt capital has a further advantage over equity capital from the point of view of the firm. This advantage relates to the differential tax treatment of interest payments on debt and dividend payments on equity. In many countries, including the UK, the interest payments on debt are said to be 'tax-deductible', which means that interest payments are deducted from total income to arrive at the taxable income of the company. In contrast, dividend payments are not tax-deductible. Thus, two companies with identical operating incomes, but which differ in terms of their level of debt will have different taxable incomes and, therefore, after-tax incomes. This tax deductibility of debt payments means that debt capital provides a 'tax shield' which is not provided by equity capital and thus further lowers the (after-tax) cost of debt from the point of view of the firm.

The fact that debt capital has a lower cost than equity capital has raised the question of whether a firm can lower its overall cost of capital and, hence, its discount rate for investment appraisal purposes by changing the mix of debt and equity which it uses. The mix of debt and equity is known as the 'capital structure' of the firm. Before we go on to consider whether it is possible to alter the discount rate by changing the proportions of debt and equity used, it is helpful to consider more fully the costs of equity and debt capital.

The cost of equity capital

As we stated in the introduction to this chapter, the cost of capital and the rate of return are two sides of the same coin. Thus in thinking about the cost of equity capital it is helpful to give consideration to the returns which equity holders receive from the ownership of equity. We saw above in deriving equation (9.5) that while the returns to equity holders comes in the form of dividend payments and capital gains, in practice we can think of returns as being made up of the discounted flow of all future dividends. While this is a helpful way of considering the returns to shareholders, we really need a measure of returns in percentage terms, i.e. we need a measure of the rate of return on equity. In equation (9.5), the discount rate k_e is the rate of return to shareholders (or alternatively, the cost of equity capital to the firm). In practice we can observe the price of a firm's shares and we can make a reasonable estimate of the future dividend flow, at least for a number of years ahead. If we can estimate dividends for all future years then we would be able to calculate the firm's cost of equity capital. While it may be unreasonable to estimate all future dividends, it is possible to arrive at a measure of the cost of capital relatively easily in two situations: where dividends are constant and where dividends are not constant but grow at a constant rate. In either of these circumstances it is possible to quite easily determine the cost of equity capital or the required rate of return to equity holders. To begin with, let us work on the basis that dividends are constant. Thus next year's dividend level will be the same as last year's and the same as all subsequent dividends. In this situation, it is possible to simplify equation (9.5) to arrive at the following valuation model. (This simplification is the result of mathematical manipulation, the mechanics of which it is not necessary to understand. However, given a constant level of dividends, we have, in effect, a perpetuity and the derivation of equation (2.7), which is shown in the appendix to Chapter 2, is identical to the derivation of the following equation):

$$P_0 = \frac{D}{k_e} . \qquad (9.6)$$

All terms are as previously defined, although in this case we do not need to differentiate between dividends in different years because they are all at the same level. Given that we can observe the values of P_0 and D, we can easily estimate the value of k_e. The cost of capital can be calculated be rearranging equation (9.6):

$$k_e = \frac{D_1}{P_0} . \qquad (9.7)$$

For example, if the constant level of dividends is 20p and the current price of the share is £1.25 then the value of k_e is $0.2/1.25 = 0.16$ or 16%.

In practice, dividends are not usually constant from year to year. However, it is often the case that dividends grow year on year and that the rate of growth is fairly constant. Where it is the case that dividends do grow at a constant rate we can again identify a much more simple share valuation equation, as shown in equation (9.8) (again, this simplification is the result of mathematical manipulation, the mechanics of which it is not necessary to understand):

$$P_0 = \frac{D_1}{(k_e - g)}, \qquad (9.8)$$

where g is the annual growth rate of dividends. Again it is possible to rearrange the equation to obtain a value for k_e:

$$k_e = \frac{D_0(1 + g)}{P_0} + g = \frac{D_1}{P_0} + g \qquad (9.9)$$

For example, if the current share price is £2.50, the value of this year's dividend is 30p and the growth rate of dividends is 5%, then next year's dividend will be 31.5p and the value of k_e will be $0.315/2.5 + 0.05 = 17.6\%$.

While dividends will not grow constantly in perpetuity, this simpified model does provide us with a means of obtaining an approximate measure of the cost of equity capital for a firm. Clearly, in an all-equity-financed firm the calculated value of k_e will be the appropriate discount rate. However, when the firm is financed by a mix of debt and equity it is necessary also to consider the cost of debt capital.

The cost of debt capital

To understand how the cost of debt capital is determined we must consider the valuation of loan stock. As with equity stock, the owners of loan stock can sell the stock to other purchasers through the capital markets. When they do this, the right to the interest payments and capital repayment passes to the new owner of the stock. However, as interest rates change, so too will the market value (as opposed to the face value) of the stock. For example, consider again the loan stock mentioned above which was issued in 1997 in units of £100 (i.e. the face value is £100) and which pays £8 per annum until the year 2012, at which point the £100 face value is repaid. Such a stock is known as a 'redeemable debenture' because it has a date at which the principal will be repaid or redeemed. Let us assume that the stock is sold in 1997 for £100 (i.e. it is sold at face value) at the time the company issues the debenture. At this point the owner of the stock has a right to interest payments of £8 per year for the next 15 years, plus the repayment of the principal after 15 years. The cost of debt at the time of issue is equal to the discount rate which equates the £100 paid out now (at the time of purchase) with the discounted income flow of £8 per year for 15 years plus £100 in the year 2012. Thus the cost of debt capital, k_d, is found in this case by solving for k_d in the following equation (the calculation is undertaken in exactly the same way as the IRR was calculated in Chapter 4):

$$100 = \frac{8}{(1 + k_d)} + \frac{8}{(1 + k_d)^2} + \frac{8}{(1 + k_d)^3} + \ldots + \frac{8}{(1 + k_d)^{15}} + \frac{100}{(1 + k_d)^{15}} . \quad (9.10)$$

In this case the cost of debt capital is equal to the interest rate on the face value and is 8%. However, if interest rates rise and a holder of the debt capital wishes to sell the loan stock he or she will not be able to sell the stock on the capital markets at the face value of the stock. For example, if interest rates rise substantially and new loan stock is being issued by companies with the same level of risk with an interest payment of £12 per annum, then the debt holder will only be able to sell the original loan stock if the £8 annual payments plus the repayment of £100 in 15 years' time provide a 12% rate of return. For this to happen the price of the loan stock must fall. If the rise in interest rates was immediately following the issue of the loan stock paying £8 per annum, then the price of the stock would fall to £72.76 and k_d rise to 12%:

$$72.76 = \frac{8}{(1 + k_d)} + \frac{8}{(1 + k_d)^2} + \frac{8}{(1 + k_d)^3} + \ldots + \frac{8}{(1 + k_d)^{15}} + \frac{100}{(1 + k_d)^{15}} .$$

However, in practice interest rates and the price of bonds will vary throughout the life of the loan stock. Even though the firm has issued stock with an annual interest payment of £8, 8% is not the relevant value of k_d when the price of stock changes, since the market value of the stock has changed and therefore the cost of debt capital has also changed. If the company wished to issue new stock it could not do so with an annual interest payment of £8. Rather, it would have to offer interest payments which are in line with current market rates. Thus, the cost of debt capital is found by finding the value of k_d which solves an equation similar to equation (9.10), but taking account of the market value of the loan stock and the total interest payments and capital repayments to be made. For example, if in the year 2002 the loan stock is selling for £61.35 then the cost of debt capital is found by finding the value of k_d which solves the following equation:

$$61.35 = \frac{8}{(1 + k_d)} + \frac{8}{(1 + k_d)^2} + \frac{8}{(1 + k_d)^3} + \ldots + \frac{8}{(1 + k_d)^{10}} + \frac{100}{(1 + k_d)^{10}} .$$

In this case the cost of debt capital has risen to 16%. More generally, the cost of debt capital is found by solving for k_d in the following equation:

$$V_b = \frac{I}{(1 + k_d)} + \frac{I}{(1 + k_d)^2} + \frac{I}{(1 + k_d)^3} + \ldots + \frac{I}{(1 + k_d)^n} + \frac{R}{(1 + k_d)^n}. \quad (9.11)$$

where V_b is the market value of the bond, I is the annual interest payment, R is the capital repayment and n is the number of years until the bond is redeemed.

Finding the value of k_d which solves equation (9.11) is the appropriate way to determine the cost of debt capital when the loan stock is redeemable. If the loan stock has no fixed redemption date it is known as 'irredeemable' and the cost of debt capital is simply the interest payment divided by the market value of the stock:

$$k_d = \frac{I}{V_b}. \quad (9.12)$$

Thus, for example, if the market value of the bond is £64 and the annual interest payment is £8 then the cost of debt capital is $8/64 = 0.125$ or 12.5%.

When interest payments are tax-deductible, the cost of debt capital calculation must reflect the fact that there is a tax shield on debt. In particular, the interest payment to be included in the calculation of the cost of capital should reflect the savings in taxation. For example, consider the case of the above irredeemable debenture which is selling for £64 and which pays annual interest payments of £8. Let us assume that the interest payment can be deducted from total income for tax purposes and that as a result taxable income is reduced by £8. If the rate of tax which the company faces is 40%, then the company's tax bill will be reduced by £8 × 40% = £3.20. Thus, the actual (net) cost of the debt to the firm is only £4.80 (calculated as £8 − £3.20) per £100 face value per year. It is the figure of £4.80 which should be included as the value of I in equation (9.12) and the cost of debt capital will be:

$$k_d = \frac{4.8}{64} = 0.075 \text{ or } 7.5\%.$$

More generally with taxation the cost of debt for irredeemables is:

$$k_d = \frac{I(1 - t)}{V_b}. \quad (9.13)$$

where t is the tax rate.

Similarly, for redeemable debentures, the value of I to be used in equation (9.11) must also be adjusted to reflect the tax shield which is offered. Thus each value of I in equation (9.11) must be multiplied by $(1 - t)$ before the after-tax cost of debt capital can be determined. For example, returning to the example of redeemable debt used earlier, the annual interest payments are £8 and the value of the bond was £61.35. If the tax rate is 40%, then the value for the net interest payments should be adjusted to reflect the tax saving. Thus, rather than using a figure of £8, the appropriate figure to use is again £4.80, calculated as $I(1 - t)$. The formula can then be used to determine the value of k_d:

$$61.35 = \frac{4.8}{(1 + k_d)} + \frac{4.8}{(1 + k_d)^2} + \frac{4.8}{(1 + k_d)^3} + \ldots + \frac{4.8}{(1 + k_d)^{10}} + \frac{100}{(1 + k_d)^{10}}.$$

Thus, the value of k_d is 11.5%. More generally, the cost of debt for redeemables is calculated as:

$$V_b = \frac{I(1 - t)}{(1 + k_d)} + \frac{I(1 - t)}{(1 + k_d)^2} + \frac{I(1 - t)}{(1 + k_d)^3} + \ldots + \frac{I(1 - t)}{(1 + k_d)^n} + \frac{R}{(1 + k_d)^n}. \qquad (9.14)$$

Thus, we can see that the cost of debt is determined by the annual interest payments due, the amount to be repaid at the redemption date, the tax rate which the company faces and the *market value* of the bond. The first two of these are stated in the terms of the loan, the third is easily observable from tax information and the final term can be readily obtained from the financial press. Once these four terms are known it is possible for the company to determine its cost of debt capital.

THE POOL OF FUNDS CONCEPT AND THE WEIGHTED AVERAGE COST OF CAPITAL

We have now established how to determine the cost of debt capital and the cost of equity capital for a firm. The cost of debt capital has been calculated not on the basis of the return on the face value of the debt, but rather the return on the market value of the bond. This is because when we are considering a new investment opportunity it is the rate of return *currently* required which is of relevance, and not the rate of interest payable at the time the debt was issued. Similarly, the cost of equity capital is calculated with reference to the market value of equity, as we have seen. However, when calculating the cost of capital for individual projects, we should not base this calculation on one particular source of capital. In practice companies have a pool of funds available for investment purposes and this pool is made up of a mixture of debt and equity. Whenever new capital is raised, for example by a new issue of loan stock or the retaining of earnings for reinvestment, this new capital is in effect added to the pool of available funds. Even when capital is raised because a particular project is being undertaken, the capital is absorbed into the pool of funds of the company and the project is funded from the pool. In calculating the cost of capital for a project it is the cost of this pool of funds which should be considered and it is therefore necessary to calculate a weighted average cost of capital, taking account of the costs of debt *and* equity capital and of their relative weights in the pool of funds.

The weighted average cost of capital (WACC)

As the name suggests, the weighted average cost of capital (WACC) takes an average of the individual costs of capital. In calculating the average figure the WACC weights the individual costs of capital by the relative values of debt and equity in the overall capital structure. Thus, for example, if the capital structure of a company consists of 75% equity and 25% debt, then the weight attached to the cost of equity capital is 0.75, while that attached to the cost of debt capital is 0.25. The question is, 'How are the weights determined?' As was the case when considering the value of k_d, it is the market values of equity and debt which are important in determining the weights. Thus, once again, we do not consider nominal or face values, since these do not represent the current values which people are willing to pay for equity or debt in the company. The total value of a company, V, consists of the market value of debt capital, D, and the market value of equity, E. Thus,

$$V = D + E.$$

Hence, if the value of equity is £800,000 and the value of debt is £200,000 then the total value of the company is £1,000,000. In determining the WACC we need to weight the costs of debt and equity capital by the values D/V (in this case, 0.2) and E/V (in this case, 0.8). In general the WACC is given by the following formula:

$$WACC = (D/V)\, k_d + (E/V)\, k_e \qquad (9.15)$$

So, in this case, if k_e is 20% and k_d is 12%, then the WACC is

$$WACC = (0.2) \times (0.12) + (0.8) \times (0.2) = 0.184 \text{ or } 18.4\%.$$

This would be the discount rate to use in any capital appraisal calculation.

The WACC is a very useful concept which provides decision makers with a useful means for calculating the discount rate for investment appraisal purposes. However, the decision maker must be aware of the circumstances in which the WACC is appropriate. There are three conditions which must be met if the WACC is to be used. First, the project under consideration must be marginal in the sense that it is of small size relative to the company as a whole. Second, the project should have the same level of risk as the company as a whole. In this case we are talking about the level of *systematic* risk. As we saw when considering the CAPM, the higher the level of systematic risk, the higher the required rate of return. Thus, it is reasonable to assume that the WACC calculated for the firm as it is currently constituted (i.e. without the project now under consideration) will only be suitable for the new project being considered if the new project has the same level of systematic risk as the company as a whole. Third, the financing of the new project should not lead to a significant change in the capital structure of the firm, i.e. in the mix of debt and equity. This is because it is possible that changing the capital structure will lead to a change in the WACC. For example, as the capital structure changes, so too do the weights attached to k_e and k_d. Similarly, as the level of debt in the company increases equity holders face increased financial risk, which will lead them to demand a higher rate of return, thus again possibly leading to a change in the WACC. If any of these conditions do not hold then we run into the problem that the WACC calculated is inappropriate for use as a discount rate. While these conditions are clearly not met in all circumstances, it is often the case that they are approximately true and, hence, the WACC is a very useful tool in practice. In most cases it is not unreasonable to assume that the project is marginal to the company as a whole. Similarly, while a project may not be of exactly the same level of risk as the company as a whole, in many situations the company undertakes projects which are in the same line of business as the existing projects of the company and thus the level of risk is very similar. While the third condition is less often fulfilled, because the debt–equity mix does change with new projects, it is often the case that the change is only temporary. In practice, many companies have a target ratio for debt to equity. While this will not always be met in the short run, the ratio is fairly constant in the medium-to-long run.

The discussion to date suggests that in many situations the WACC will provide an appropriate measure of the discount rate to use in NPV calculations, while recognizing that the WACC is not a perfect measure, but rather an approximate measure of the true discount rate. Clearly, where the conditions obviously do not hold, for example when a company moves into a new line of business which has a very different level of systematic risk to existing business, then the WACC is not an appropriate measure of the discount rate. In these circumstances, the WACC is not appropriate and the decision maker would be better advised to calculate the discount rate using the CAPM approach.

IS THERE AN OPTIMAL CAPITAL STRUCTURE?

One final issue which should be briefly considered relates to the question of whether the company can reduce its WACC, and hence increase firm value by changing the mix of debt and equity. If the WACC can be reduced this will automatically lead to there being an increase in firm value, since the WACC is the value which is used to discount the future cash flows of the company to determine the value of the company. The fact that debt capital is cheaper than equity capital, due to debt capital being less risky from the point of view of the providers of funds and it having tax advantages, has led to considerable debate about whether there is an optimal capital structure which minimizes the WACC. A full discussion of this issue is beyond the scope of this book, since it involves detailed theoretical arguments dating back some 40 years and which are still continuing to this day. These arguments cover a wide range of issues, reflecting not only the advantages which debt capital offers, but also its disadvantages. For example, since debt capital increases financial risk, equity holders are likely to demand a higher return when more debt is taken on. Similarly, increased debt capital increases the possibility of bankruptcy and there are normally large costs associated with bankruptcy. For example, when assets are liquidated following bankruptcy, they are usually sold for only a percentage of their value in a going concern. These bankruptcy costs mean that increasing the level of debt has serious disadvantages. The issues involved in deciding whether there exists an optimal capital structure led Lumby to state:

all we can say is that it would appear that the financing decision may be of some importance, in so far as a company's capital structure can have both beneficial and detrimental effects on its total market value . . . . However, the exact nature of the relationship in real life between a company's gearing level, its total market value and the costs of its various types of capital remains unclear.

(1991, p. 388)

In spite of a lack of clarity about the precise way in which the WACC changes as the level of gearing changes, nonetheless, the WACC provides a very useful means for determining the discount rate to be used in many circumstances. It is however, important that the decision maker be aware of the conditions under which the WACC 'works' and gives careful consideration to its use.

SUMMARY AND KEY POINTS

This chapter has examined the issue of how to determine the discount rate for investment appraisal purposes from the point of view of the cost of funds, rather than from the point of view of the rate of return required by the providers of funds. It has been shown that these two concepts are essentially two sides of the same coin, and that under certain circumstances the WACC provides an appropriate means by which to calculate the discount rate. However, it has also been shown that there are problems with the calculation of the WACC and its use for projects which differ in terms of systematic risk from the company as a whole, or where undertaking the project may lead to a substantial change in the gearing of the firm. The key points from this chapter are:

- The cost of capital method for determining the discount rate gives direct consideration to the cost of the funds which will be used for investment. This approach to determining the discount rate is of considerable use and has great intuitive appeal, focusing as it does on the cost of funds used to finance the investment.
- The ratio of debt to equity in the mix of capital in the firm is known as the 'gearing ratio' or as the 'level of gearing'.
- There are essentially two sources of long-term finance for investment purposes: namely, equity capital and debt capital. The holders of equity capital own the company and this form of capital represents the risk capital of the company. The holders of equity capital are said to have a 'residual claim' on the assets of the company.
- The providers of debt capital do not own the company, rather, they purchase a debenture which involves them *lending* money to the firm. In return for lending this money, debenture holders have a right to certain guaranteed payments during the life of the bond. Debt holders are said to have a 'prior claim' on the assets of the company.
- Debt capital is less risky than equity capital and, therefore, the cost of debt capital is lower than the cost of equity capital.
- The dividend share valuation model provides us with a means of obtaining an approximate measure of the cost of equity capital, k_e, for a firm.
- In an all-equity-financed firm the calculated value of k_e will be the

appropriate discount rate. However, when the firm is financed by a mix of debt and equity it is necessary to also consider the cost of debt capital.

- The cost of debt capital requires account to be taken of the market value of the loan stock and the total interest payments and capital repayments to be made. The nominal interest rate on the face value of the bond is not the cost of debt capital, except where the bond is selling at face value, which rarely happens.
- When interest payments are tax-deductible, the cost of debt capital calculation must reflect the fact that there is a tax shield on debt. In particular, the interest payment to be included in the calculation of the cost of capital should reflect the savings in taxation.
- When calculating the cost of capital for individual projects, we should not base this calculation on one particular source of capital. In practice companies have a pool of funds available for investment purposes and this pool is made up of a mixture of debt and equity. In calculating the cost of capital for a project it is the cost of this pool of funds which should be considered.
- The weighted average cost of capital (WACC) is the appropriate measure, since it takes an average of the individual costs of capital. The WACC is a very useful concept which provides decision makers with a useful means for calculating the discount rate for investment appraisal purposes. However, in certain circumstances the WACC is not an appropriate measure of the discount rate.
- It is important that the decision maker be aware of the conditions under which the WACC 'works' and give careful consideration to its use.

WORKED EXAMPLE

A firm wishes to calculate its WACC to use in an investment appraisal calculation. The following information is obtained (the information does not take account of the proposed project):

(a) The current year's dividend, which has just been paid, was 20p. Next year's dividend is expected to be 24p and dividends are then expected to grow at an annual rate of 6%.

(b) The current share price is £3.20 and there are one million shares issued.

(c) The company issued debt capital some time ago with a face value of £100 and with annual interest payments of £10. The loan stock is now selling for £80 and there will be a further eight annual interest payments and a capital repayment in eight year's time of £100.

(d) When the loan stock was issued it had a total face value of £1,000,000.

(e) The firm will receive a tax shield of 30% on interest payments.

What is the weighted average cost of capital for this firm?

Answers:

To answer this question it is first necessary to calculate the cost of equity capital and the cost of debt capital. From point (a) we can see that as from next year (i.e. year 1 onwards) dividend growth is constant. We can therefore use the constant growth model as shown in equation (9.9) to determine the cost of equity capital. (The value of this year's dividends which have recently been paid are irrelevant in determining the cost of equity capital since that payment is in the past.)

$$k_e = (D_1/P_0) + g = (0.24/3.2) + 0.06 = 0.135 \text{ or } 13.5\%.$$

The cost of debt capital is calculated by solving for k_d in equation (9.14). Since the company has a tax shield of 30% on the debt interest payments, its net interest payments per £100 face value is the total interest payment of £10 less the tax saving of £3. Thus the net figure of £7 should be included as the net interest payment and we solve for k_d in the following equation:

$$80 = 7/(1 + k_d) + 7/(1 + k_d)^2 + 7/(1 + k_d)^3 + \ldots + 7/(1 + k_d)^8 + 100/(1 + k_d)^8.$$

By trial and error (or by using a computer package) we can calculate that k_d is equal to 10.9% (this figure is calculated in exactly the same way as the IRR in Chapter 4).

We must now calculate the weights to be applied to the two costs of capital. The current market value of the equity capital is 1,000,000 (the number of shares) times the current share price of £3.20. Thus $E = £3,200,000$. The current market value of the debt capital is £800,000 (since the original value was £1,000,000 and each £100 face value bond is now selling for £80). Thus $D = £800,000$ and $V = D + E = £4,000,000$.

We have seen that:

$$WACC = (D/V) k_d + (E/V) k_e$$

and therefore in this case:

$$WACC = (0.8/4) \times (0.109) + (3.2/4) \times (0.135) = 0.1298 \text{ or } 12.98\%.$$

QUESTIONS

9.1 Why can we think of the rate of return and the cost of capital as being two sides of the same coin?

9.2 Explain which providers of funds have a 'prior claim' and which have a 'residual claim' on the assets of the firm.

9.3 From the point of view of the cost of equity capital, does it matter whether that capital comes from a new share issue or from retained earnings? Why or why not?

9.4 What are the reasons why debt capital in a firm typically has a lower cost of capital than does equity capital in the same firm?

9.5 Under what circumstances is the WACC an appropriate measure of the discount rate for a project? Are these circumstances likely to hold in practice?

10 DEALING WITH INFLATION, TAXATION AND THE LEASE-VERSUS-BUY DECISION

Introduction

In first considering the main techniques available for appraising investment opportunities, we began by making simplifying assumptions in order to gain an understanding of the techniques. For example, in discussing NPV and IRR we first assumed that we knew the outcomes of investment decisions with certainty, in that there was no doubt as to the cash flows associated with each project. The problems caused by a lack of uncertainty over the actual values of cash flows from a project have been extensively discussed in earlier chapters. However, two other simplifying assumptions which were made in the early chapters of this book have not been considered. In particular, we have not given detailed consideration to the problems caused by inflation and taxation. In discussing the nature of the cash flows to be included in any appraisal it was stated in Chapter 1 that 'accounting conventions should not impact upon the figures included in the investment appraisal calculations, except to the extent that they impact upon actual cash flows (for example, through their impact on the level of taxation the company must pay)'. However, in the discussion to date, no consideration has been given to the role of taxation. Similarly, in Chapter 2 it was stated that 'we will initially ignore the problems caused by inflation by assuming that the economy in which the decision maker is operating has a zero inflation rate, i.e. £1 today buys the same amount of goods as £1 in the future'. Clearly, this assumption is unrealistic and we need to give attention to the problems which arise when the assumption is relaxed. In this chapter we discuss the problems caused for the investment appraisal process by the existence of taxation and inflation. We also set out the means by which decision makers can address these problems and take them into account in the decision-making process. The fact that these issues are not being discussed until late in the book, does not mean that they are trivial issues. However, as we shall see, they are issues which can readily be taken into account in the investment appraisal process. In addition, in considering investment opportunities we have only given attention to those situations in which the project involves purchase of an asset to undertake the investment. In practice, it is sometimes possible to lease an asset, rather than purchase the asset. This chapter will, therefore, briefly consider the lease-versus-buy decision.

All modern economies are characterized by changes in the purchasing power of money. The goods which can currently be purchased for £1, are very likely to cost more than £1 in the future. For example, the price of petrol has increased frequently in recent years and will continue to do so in the future. While some goods become cheaper through time (for example, video recorders have fallen in price in recent years), typically, most goods become more expensive through time. This general increase in the price of goods through time reduces the purchasing power of money, and such a general increase in the price level is known as 'inflation'. Thus, the assumption made in Chapter 2, that £1 today buys the same amount of goods as £1 in the future, is not correct, and this fact needs to be taken into account in considering investment opportunities. Although the UK has recently experienced a period of relatively low inflation, nonetheless the erosion of purchasing power through time can be significant. For example, an inflation rate of only 3% per annum will mean that goods which cost £1 today will cost £1.34 in ten years' time, an increase of over a third.

The reason why inflation is of importance to the investment appraisal process can be seen by considering again the definition of investment given in Chapter 1:

An investment can be defined as any act which involves the sacrifice of an immediate and certain level of consumption in exchange for the expectation of an increase in future consumption.

In this definition, it is not the *amount of money* which is considered important, but the *level of consumption*. A trade-off is being made between consumption now and consumption in the future. In making such a trade-off, it is necessary to consider how much goods can be purchased at different points in time and thus if the purchasing power of money changes we need to take this into account. The importance of the changing purchasing power of money and the problems caused by inflation are best illustrated by an example.

Consider a position in which there is zero inflation and where an investor is willing to invest £1,000 in a project provided that he or she receives £1,150 in one year's time. Thus, the investor's discount rate or required rate of return in the absence of inflation is 15% (£1,000 × 1.15 = £1,150). The investor, therefore, requires 15% extra purchasing power to compensate for delaying consumption by one year. Now consider a situation in which there is inflation of 10%. In such a world, the investor will still be willing to undertake the investment of £1,000 provided that he or she receives an extra 15% purchasing power in a year. However, it is now the case that in one year it will cost £1,100 to purchase what currently costs £1,000 due to the effects of inflation. If the investor is only offered £1,150 in a year's time for giving up £1,000 now, then the extra purchasing power being offered is much less than 15%. Indeed, the investor is only being offered an extra £50 worth of purchasing power (£1,150 − £1,100) which represents only about 4.5% extra consumption (£50/£1,100 × 100). To give the investor an extra 15% purchasing power requires that the investor receive

£1,265 in a year's time (£1,100 × 1.15). Thus, the rate of return on the investment must be 26.5% in money terms [(1,265 − 1,000)/1,000 × 100] to make the investment attractive to the investor.

This example illustrates a problem which is encountered in the face of inflation: namely, there are two rates of interest. First, there is a purchasing-power rate of interest, which in this case is 15%. Second, there is a money rate of interest, which in this case is 26.5%. The purchasing-power rate of interest is also known as the 'real rate of interest', while the money rate of interest is also known as the 'market rate of interest' or the 'nominal rate of interest'. The relationship between the real rate of interest, r, the nominal rate of interest, n, and the inflation rate, i, is shown below:

$$(1 + n) = (1 + r) \times (1 + i).$$

In the above example, n = 26.5% or 0.265, r = 15% or 0.15 and i = 10% or 0.1:

$$(1 + 0.265) = (1 + 0.15) \times (1 + 0.1).$$

The problem for the decision maker is which of these two interest rates should be used as the discount rate in the appraisal of the investment. Clearly, the NPV which is calculated for a given set of cash inflows would be significantly affected by the interest rate used. For example, a project which requires an initial investment of £2,000 and which generates cash inflows over two years of £1,350 would have an NPV of +£195 if the discount rate were 15%, but it would have an NPV of (−£89) if the discount rate used were 26.5%. It is, therefore, obvious that the choice of which of the two discount rates is to be used is crucial to the investment decision process. So, should the decision maker use the real rate of interest or the nominal rate of interest as the discount rate?

The answer to this question depends upon the way in which the cash flows which are to be included in the investment appraisal have been calculated. In particular, have they been calculated taking account of inflation or have the effects of inflation been excluded? If the cash flows have been calculated without taking account of the effects of inflation, then the real rate of interest should be used. If they have been calculated taking inflation into account then the nominal rate should be used. Let us again consider an example. Suppose an investment project is being suggested which will require a capital outlay of £20,000 and which is expected to generate sales of 1,500 units of a new product in each of the next three years and nothing thereafter. The company estimates that the product will be able to sell this number of units each year if the price is £7 in current prices (i.e. ignoring the effects of inflation). Thus, the current-value cash flows will be 1,500 × 7 = £10,500 in each of three years. The real rate of interest is 15% and the expected inflation rate is 10% per annum over the life of the project. Thus, the nominal rate of interest is 26.5%. While the current-value cash flows are £10,500 per annum, inflation will cause the cash flows to differ from this figure. In year 1 the selling price will rise by 10% from £7 to £7.70. In year 2, the selling price will rise by a further 10% to £8.47 and in year 3 it will rise by a further 10% to £9.32. Thus, the *actual* cash flows, if sales are 1,500 units per annum, will be £11,550 in year 1, £12,705 in year 2 and £13,980 in year 3.

The decision maker can now calculate the NPV of the project by one of two means: *either* using current-value cash flows and discounting these at the real rate of interest, *or* using actual cash flows and discounting these at the nominal rate of interest. The NPVs using these two methods are shown below:

Discounting current-value cash flows using the real rate of interest:

$$\text{NPV} = -20{,}000 + \frac{10{,}500}{1.15} + \frac{10{,}500}{1.15^2} + \frac{10{,}500}{1.15^3} = \pounds3{,}974.$$

Discounting actual cash flows using the nominal rate of interest:

$$\text{NPV} = -20{,}000 + \frac{11{,}500}{1.265} + \frac{12{,}705}{1.265^2} + \frac{13{,}980}{1.265^3} = \pounds3{,}976.$$

The example shows that the calculated NPV is the same whichever method is used (actually there is a difference of £2 due to rounding effects – this is due to the price in year 3 being calculated as £9.32, when in fact an increase of 10% on £8.47 gives a price of £9.317). Hence, it is possible to use either rate of interest provided that the decision maker is consistent in the use of the rate of interest and the method of calculating cash flows. If current-value cash flows are used (i.e. excluding inflation), then the real rate of interest should be used. In this case inflation is not being taken into account in any of the calculations. If inflation-adjusted (or actual) cash flows are being used then the nominal rate of interst should be used. In this case inflation is taken into account in all calculations. The use of either method is acceptable. However, the decision maker must ensure that he or she does not mix up real values with nominal values. Using such a mix would be inappropriate and could lead to inaccurate advice.

While both approaches are equally acceptable, it is perhaps advisable to use nominal values. This method can be superior for two reasons. First, it is possible that not all cash flows need to be adjusted by the same rate of price increase. For example, while sale price may be expected to rise by 10% per annum, energy costs may only be expected to rise by 8% and labour costs by 7%. By using nominal values, the different impacts on each component of the net cash-flow forecast can be taken into account. Second, when money is being borrowed at a specific rate of interest, the figure quoted will take account of expected inflation and is, therefore, a nominal rate. Thus, if real values are to be used, it would be necessary to extract the inflation rate from the quoted interest rate to determine the real rate of interest.

While it is clear that the existence of inflation causes a potential problem for the decision maker considering investment opportunities, it is also clear from the discussion above that the problem can be readily addressed. The decision maker must ensure that a consistent approach is used in calculating a figure for the NPV. Either, cash flows and discount rates should be used that reflect the impact of inflation or cash flows and discount rates should be used that exclude the impact of inflation. Either is appropriate, but the decision maker must ensure that a mix of real and nominal figures is not used.

Taxation is an important issue which needs to be given full consideration when potential investment projects are being appraised. In Chapter 1 we stated that 'the assessment of alternative investment opportunities should be undertaken with the objective of maximizing the wealth of the shareholders'. In assessing investment opportunities with the aim of maximizing shareholder wealth, it is the after-tax wealth of shareholders which is of paramount importance. The purpose of maximizing shareholder wealth is to allow investors to choose a consumption pattern which gives them maximum satisfaction. Since shareholders can only purchase goods for consumption after taxes have been paid, it is necessary to take into account the taxation implications of investment decisions.

In order to fully consider the impact of taxation on investment opportunities it is necessary to have a detailed understanding of the tax system under which the company is liable to pay tax. Any such tax system is subject to periodic change, with the rates of tax changing through time and the tax reliefs available to companies changing also. Not only is it beyond the scope of this book to set out a particular tax system and its implications for investment appraisal, but also setting out the details of the tax system would be largely futile, since those details are likely to change fairly rapidly. For this reason, the discussion of taxation given here will concentrate on broad principles which we need to bear in mind, rather than setting out specific taxation details. The decision maker considering the impact of taxation on investment opportunities will need to obtain specialist tax advice to fully understand how tax affects the desirability or otherwise of a particular investment.

Investment appraisal can be affected by taxation in three main ways. First, any desirable investment opportunity is likely to have an impact on the level of reported profit of the company. The net cash inflows resulting from an investment opportunity will change reported profits, which in turn will lead to a change in the level of tax to be paid. It is, therefore, important that the decision maker be fully aware of any additional taxation on profits which will result from undertaking the investment opportunity. Since tax payments are actual cash flows they must be taken into account in determining the net cash flows resulting from a project. However, as with all cash flows, it is important that the flow be attributed to the correct time period. In other words, not only does the level of extra taxation which is due need to be taken into account, but also the time at which the tax liability arises needs to be considered. In many countries, the tax will only become due in the year *after* the financial year in which the increased liability has arisen. For example, consider a project which leads to an increase in taxable profit of £60,000 in years 1–3, where the rate of profits tax is 24% and tax is due one year after the end of the financial year. The cash flows to be included in any investment appraisal in respect of tax payments should be £14,400 (£60,000 × 24%) in each of years 2–4. Thus, even though the liability arose in years 1–3, payment only occurs in years 2–4 and it is in the cash flows for these years that the tax outflow should be included. Given the time value of money, including the correct figure in the wrong year could have a substantial impact on the NPV of the project. For example, with a discount rate of 18%, including the figure of £14,400 in each of years 1–3 would have the following negative impact on the NPV:

$$\text{Effect on NPV} = \frac{-14,000}{1.18} - \frac{14,000}{1.18^2} - \frac{14,000}{1.18^3} = -£31,310.$$

However, the correct effect, taking account of the fact that the payments are not due until years 2–4, is:

$$\text{Effect on NPV} = \frac{-14,400}{1.18^2} - \frac{14,400}{1.18^3} - \frac{14,400}{1.18^4} = -£26,534.$$

This represents a difference of £4,776. Thus, it is clear that the timing at which any tax payment must be made is of significance.

The second way in which taxation can impact on the investment appraisal calculation relates to the way in which any capital expenditure can be set against profits for tax purposes. In many countries capital expenditure can be set against taxable profits through a system of writing-down allowances (WDA). With such a system, a proportion of the expenditure is set against taxable profits each year. For example, consider where the WDA is 25% of the cost of any plant and machinery in the first year, followed by a further 25% of the reducing balance in each subsequent year. Let the cost of plant and machinery in year 0 be £120,000. In the first year the WDA will be 25% of £120,000, which is £30,000. This WDA will reduce taxable profits by £30,000 in the first year. In the second year, the WDA will be 25% of the reduced balance. The reduced balance is the original cost (£120,000) minus the WDA to date (£30,000). Thus the WDA for the second year is 25% of £90,000, which is £22,500. The third year, WDA will be 25% of £67,500 (calculated as £90,000 − £22,500), which is £16,875, and so on for future years. With a company profits tax rate of 24%, the impact on tax in each of the first three years will be a saving of £7,200 in the first year (calculated as 24% of £30,000), a saving of £5,400 in the second year (calculated as 24% of £22,500), and a saving of £4,050 in the third year (calculated as 24% of £16,875). Once again it is necessary to take the timing of the change in tax liability into account. It is also possible that when an asset is finally sold, there will be a balancing charge for tax purposes which may lead to additional tax being due. Again, expert advice is required to take account of this possibility.

The third way in which tax can impact on investment appraisal calculations is through its impact on the cost of capital or the discount rate. For example, interest on debt is often tax-deductible. This impact was discussed in the previous chapter in relation to the cost of debt capital.

In considering investment opportunities and in determining the NPV of any potential project it is essential that all taxation implications are taken into account. Failure to do so can greatly affect the NPV which is calculated and lead to an incorrect decision being taken about the desirability or otherwise of the investment opportunity.

In a situation in which it is possible to lease an asset to undertake an investment project, the decision maker should consider whether leasing is preferable to purchase. With a lease, one party (the lessor) purchases the asset to be used in the project and allows another party (the lessee) to use the asset in return for a series of payments. The user of the asset is, therefore, not the owner of the asset, but rather rents the asset from the owner. In considering whether purchasing or leasing an asset is worthwhile, the NPV method is again appropriate. However, the two means of acquiring the use of the asset will have different associated cash flows. In particular, rather than paying for the asset at the outset, the lessee makes a series of payments to the lessor. In addition, the lease may state that it is the responsibility of the lessor to maintain the asset, reducing the cash outflows in respect of maintenance, as compared to purchasing. Similarly, at the end of the lease, the asset will return to the lessor who will then receive any residual value from selling the asset. Clearly, these differences between leasing and buying mean that the two methods of acquiring the asset will have different cash flows, and hence, different NPVs. For example, consider a company which requires the use of a particular machine. The cash flows associated with the purchase, maintenance and residual value of the asset are shown in Table 10.1 for buying the asset. The relevant cash flows for leasing are shown in Table 10.2. The discount rate is 12%. (For simplicity, assume that all other cash flows are unaffected by whether the asset is bought or leased and can therefore be ignored for consideration of the lease-versus-buy decision (e.g. sales revenue and energy and labour costs are the same irrespective of whether the asset is bought or leased).) The NPV relating to the cash flows from purchase is:

$$NPV = -21,000 - 2,232 - 1,993 + 2,491 = -£22,734$$

The NPV from the cash flows from leasing is:

$$NPV = -7,143 - 6,378 - 5,694 = -£19,215.$$

In this case the negative cash flow associated with leasing is considerably lower than that associated with purchase and it is therefore the case that leasing is preferable.

In this example we have only considered the cash flows which are different between leasing and purchasing in determining whether it is better to lease or

Table 10.1

Year	Purchase cost/ Scrap value	Maintenance cost	Net cash flow (NCF)	PV of NCF
0	(21,000)	0	(21,000)	(21,000)
1		(2,500)	(2,500)	(2,232)
2		(2,500)	(2,500)	(1,993)
3	6,000	(2,500)	3,500	2,491

Table 10.2

Year	Cash flow	PV of cash flow
0	0	0
1	(8,000)	(7,143)
2	(8,000)	(6,378)
3	(8,000)	(5,694)

purchase. In practice, of course, it is necessary to consider *all* cash flows, since it is possible that while leasing is preferable to purchase, neither leasing nor purchase leads to a positive NPV. Thus, simply because one of either leasing or purchasing is preferable does not mean that the project should go ahead. The decision maker must decide not only which method of acquiring the use of the asset is preferable, but also whether acquisition of the use of the asset is worthwhile at all. In addition, there may be other problems associated with evaluating the leasing option. For example, it is possible that there are differences in tax treatment between leasing and buying. The decision maker needs to be aware of any such problems.

SUMMARY AND KEY POINTS

In this chapter we have given attention to two key issues in investment appraisal: namely inflation and taxation. We have seen that if a figure for the NPV of a project is to have meaning it is essential that we are consistent in the treatment of inflation in determining the NPV and that cash-flow implications of the taxation system must be taken into account. Since an invesment decision can have important effects on the tax to be paid by a company and since tax represents a cash flow, it is essential that the impact of investments on the level and timing of tax payments be considered in the NPV calculation. In addition, we have briefly considered the lease-versus-purchase decision. The key points from this chapter are:

- A general increase in the price of goods through time reduces the purchasing power of money and such a general increase in the price level is known as 'inflation'.
- In considering investments, it is not the *amount of money* which is considered important, but the *level of consumption*. A trade-off must be made between consumption now and consumption in the future. In making such a trade-off, it is necessary to consider how much goods can be purchased at different points in time and thus if the purchasing power of money changes it is necessary to take this into account.
- In the face of inflation there are two rates of interest: the purchasing-power rate of interest, also known as the 'real rate of interest', and the money rate of interest, also known as the 'market rate of interest' or the 'nominal rate of interest'.

- In calculating the NPV of an investment project the decision maker must decide which of the two rates of interest to use. If the cash flows have been calculated without taking account of the effects of inflation, then the real rate of interest should be used. If they have been calculated taking inflation into account then the nominal rate should be used.
- It is possible to use either rate of interest provided that the decision maker is consistent in the use of the rate of interest and the method of calculating cash flows. However, the decision maker must ensure that he or she does not mix up real values with nominal values. Using such a mix would be inappropriate and could lead to inaccurate advice.
- Taxation is an important issue which needs to be given full consideration when potential investment projects are being appraised. In assessing investment opportunities with the aim of maximizing shareholder wealth, it is the after-tax wealth of shareholders which is of paramount importance.
- The net cash inflows resulting from an investment opportunity will change reported profits, which in turn will lead to a change in the level of tax to be paid. The decision maker must be fully aware of any additional taxation on profits which will result from undertaking the investment.
- Not only does the level of extra taxation which is due need to be taken into account, but also the time at which the tax liability arises needs to be considered.
- In many countries capital expenditure can be set against taxable profits through a system of writing-down allowances (WDA). With such a system, a proportion of the expenditure is set against taxable profits each year, leading to a reduction in tax due.
- Tax can also impact on investment appraisal calculations through its impact on the cost of capital or the discount rate. For example, in many countries debt interest is tax-deductible.
- In considering investment opportunities and in determining the NPV of any potential project it is essential that all taxation implications be taken into account.
- In a situation in which it is possible to lease an asset to undertake an investment project, the decision maker should consider whether leasing is preferable to purchase.
- Differences between leasing and buying mean that the two methods of acquiring the asset will have different cash flows, and hence, different NPVs.
- The decision maker must decide not only which method of acquiring the use of the asset is preferable, but also whether acquisition of the use of the asset is worthwhile at all.

WORKED EXAMPLE

A company is considering a new investment opportunity. It anticipates that the new project will cost £35,000, that it will generate sales of 1,000 units per year for five years and that the current-value selling price will be £10. Inflation is expected to be 5% in each of the next three years and 7% for the two years after that. The relevant real interest or discount rate is 8%. Calculate the NPV of the project using the nominal interest rate and money cash flows.

Answer:

To begin with it is helpful to calculate the selling price in money terms and the relevant discount rate in each of the next five years (the numbers are rounded to the nearest penny or to three decimal places for the discount rate).

Year	Inflation rate	Selling price	(1+Discount rate)
1	5%	$10 \times 1.05 = 10.50$	$1.08 \times 1.05 = 1.134$
2	5%	$10.50 \times 1.05 = 11.03$	$1.08^2 \times 1.05^2 = 1.286$
3	5%	$11.03 \times 1.05 = 11.58$	$1.08^3 \times 1.05^3 = 1.458$
4	7%	$11.58 \times 1.07 = 12.39$	$1.08^4 \times 1.05^3 \times 1.07 = 1.685$
5	7%	$12.39 \times 1.07 = 13.26$	$1.08^5 \times 1.05^3 \times 1.07^2 = 1.947$

By multiplying the selling price by 1,000 (the number of units to be sold) we obtain the cash flow for each year and we can now calculate the NPV:

$$NPV = \frac{10{,}500}{1.134} + \frac{11{,}030}{1.286} + \frac{11{,}580}{1.458} + \frac{12{,}390}{1.685} + \frac{13{,}260}{1.947} - 35{,}000 = £4{,}994$$

We can show that this is correct (apart from rounding errors caused by working to three decimal places) by calculating the NPV using real interest rates and current-value cash flows. The discount factor for an annual payment of £1 for five years when the discount rate is 8% can be seen from Table B to be 3.99271. Multiplying this by 10,000 (£10 × 1,000 units) gives a value of £39,927 and subtracting the initial outlay of £35,000 yields an NPV of £4,927.

QUESTIONS

10.1 Why should inflation be taken into account when appraising investment opportunities?

10.2 In the presence of inflation, there are two interest rates: the nominal rate and the real rate. Which should be used in the investment appraisal process?

10.3 What are the ways in which taxation can affect the investment appraisal process?

10.4 Explain why it might be possible for a project to be worthwhile undertaking when an asset is leased but not when the asset must be purchased.

10.5 If buying an asset is preferable in NPV terms to leasing an asset, is the purchase of the asset *necessarily* worthwhile? Why or why not?

Dealing with Inflation, Taxation and the Lease-versus-Buy Decision

11 PROJECT EVALUATION AND THE MONITORING OF PERFORMANCE

Introduction

In discussing the techniques which are available to assist the decision maker in earlier chapters, we have stressed on many occasions that the techniques can only provide a guide to the decision-making process, they do not replace the decision-making process. Great emphasis has been placed on the idea that investment appraisal techniques can inform and assist the decision maker, but they do not provide hard-and-fast decision rules. Nonetheless, it has been shown that the techniques can be of great use and do make it more likely that a well-informed decision will be taken as to which, if any, project to undertake. Having given consideration to the techniques available for undertaking an investment appraisal, to potential problems which may be encountered in using the techniques and to means by which to address those problems in earlier chapters, now we turn to the issue of what to do once the decision has been taken and the investment has begun to be implemented. It needs to be stressed that the implementation of the project does not constitute the end of the investment appraisal process. Rather, it is necessary for the decision maker to evaluate projects after they have begun and to monitor the performance of the project as it proceeds.

THE IMPLEMENTATION OF THE PROJECT

Once the decision has been taken to undertake a project, it is the responsibility of the project manager to oversee the implementation of the investment. Clearly, with many projects there will be many and varied aspects involved in the implementation of a project. For example, consider the launch of a new product which requires the building of a new factory. With such an investment there will be many dimensions to the implementation process, including, for example, the purchase of an appropriate site, the design of the factory,

contracting of the building work, the hiring of a suitable workforce, the over
seeing of that workforce, the design and marketing of the product, etc. Not onl
are there many dimensions to this process, but also the different dimensions ar
likely to be spread out over time. For example, the purchase of the site wi
come long before the marketing of the product.

While the project manager will not have direct responsibility for all aspect
of the project and may need to bring together a team for its implementatior
nonetheless, the manager needs to be aware of what is going on, of what i
required at different stages of the investment process and of whether th
timetable for implementing the project is being adhered to. Where it is no
the manager must know as quickly as possible that there is a delay and what i
the cause of the problem. In other words, the manager needs to monitor th
progress of the project and the extent to which that progress is in line with
forecasts made at the investment appraisal stage. Monitoring of the implemen
tation of the project has two main functions: to allow remedial action to b
taken, where necessary, and to gain an understanding of when and why projec
implementation differs from estimates, with a view to improving investmen
decision making in the future.

MONITORING AND REMEDIAL ACTION

The monitoring of progress requires consideration of both physical and finan
cial aspects of the project. For example, not only is it important to know that th
factory is being built to schedule, but it is also important to know what are th
costs of the building programme. Similarly, the manager needs to know
whether the planned number of units of output are being produced and sold
and also whether the sale price per unit is as predicted. Given that many
projects are complex and have many different stages, it will be necessary fo
appropriate information systems to be in place so that the manager is aware o
the progress of all aspects of the project.

Once the manager identifies delays or problems, then it is necessary to
decide whether and what remedial action is required. For example, if the leve
of sales is lower than expected, the manager should try to identify why this is
the case and what, if any, action to take. Sales can be below expectations for a
number of reasons, and the reason can be important in determining the action
to take. For example, if sales are low because a competitor has launched a
similar product with a major advertising campaign then it might be appro
priate for the firm to similarly undertake more advertising. On the other hand
if the low sales are due to an unexpected fall in consumer spending following
an unpredicted and particularly harsh budget which has increased taxes sub
stantially, then there may be little that the firm can do to increase sales. It may
then be appropriate to consider scaling down the project until there is a pick-up
in the economy. Importantly, the manager should not simply assume that the
project is proceeding as predicted. From the manager's point of view it is
important to know what is going on and the cause of any deviation from

predictions. Armed with this information, the manager can decide on appropriate action.

MONITORING AND IMPROVING FUTURE DECISION MAKING

In the example which we have just considered, the deviation in sales from the predicted level was due to changes which had not been anticipated. Decision makers can learn a great deal from these events which may be of considerable benefit for future investment appraisal. For example, it may be necessary to give much greater consideration than had previously been thought to the activities of competitors, when appraising new investment opportunities. Furthermore, it is possible that deviations from predictions are not due to external factors, but rather are due to systematic errors in forecasts at the time of the investment appraisal. It is quite possible that, for example, the sales department has a tendency to be over-optimistic and typically overestimates future sales. Similarly, the production department may have a tendency to underestimate breakdown rates of machines that it is using. By monitoring the progress of a project it may be possible for the manager to identify such tendencies and to take these into account in the appraisal of future investment opportunities.

The lessons to be learned from past investment appraisal can either come through the monitoring of the progress of the project or from a *post audit*. While there are similarities between ongoing monitoring and post audit, they differ in that post audit normally takes place after a significant amount of time has elapsed in the life of the project. The post audit should not concentrate on all parts of the project, but rather should focus on those aspects which are of most significance in determining the success or otherwise of the project. Factors which were seen to be particularly important in any sensitivity analysis which was undertaken at the investment appraisal stage may be worthy of detailed review. An important by-product of a post audit may be that if all those involved in undertaking the investment appraisal know that their forecasts are likely to be subject to close scrutiny in a future post audit, they may take greater care in making forecasts at the investment appraisal stage. Thus, for example, if the sales department knows that there will come a time when they are accountable for their sales forecasts, they may be more reticent in overestimating sales levels. On the other hand, it is also possible that post audits may lead to caution on the part of those providing forecasts, which may lead to potentially profitable projects being rejected. For example, the sales department may choose to underestimate sales, rather than be held accountable for an overestimation at a later date. It is, therefore, important that post audits be used in a constructive way and that departments be held responsible not only for being over-optimistic, but also for being unduly pessimistic. If used correctly, post audits can be an important tool for improving investment decision making.

This chapter has briefly discussed the monitoring of investment projects once they have begun to be implemented. It has been stressed that monitoring is important since it allows decision makers to understand the extent to which the progress of the project conforms to predictions. This, in turn, is important for deciding upon appropriate remedial action and for informing the investment appraisal process in the future. The key points from this chapter are:

- The implementation of an investment does not constitute the end of the appraisal process. Rather, it is necessary for the decision maker to evaluate projects after they have begun and to monitor the performance of the project as it proceeds.
- The manager needs to be aware of what is going on, of what is required at different stages of the investment process and of whether the timetable for implementing the project is being adhered to.
- Monitoring of the implementation of the project has two main functions: to allow remedial action to be taken, where necessary, and to improve investment decision making in the future.
- The monitoring of progress requires consideration of both physical and financial aspects of the project.
- It is important for the manager to know what is going on and the cause of any deviation from predictions. Such information allows the manager to decide on appropriate action.
- Post audits normally take place after a significant amount of time has elapsed in the life of the project. They allow the key features of the investment decision process to be evaluated and give the opportunity for managers to learn from deviations and to inform the decision-making process in the future.

QUESTIONS

11.1 Explain the role and importance of information in monitoring and evaluating project implementation.

11.2 What are the main functions of monitoring the implementation of a project?

11.3 If a manager determines that sales are lower than estimated, what further information would be required and what remedial action could the manager take?

11.4 Distinguish between monitoring of a project and post audit.

11.5 Why might a post audit draw on the findings of sensitivity analysis undertaken before the decision to go ahead with a project had been made?

Table A Present value of £1: $1/(1 + R)^n$

Rate (%) Period (n)	1.0	1.5	2.0	2.5	3.0	3.5	4.0	4.5	5.0	5.5	6.0	6.5	7.0
1	0.99010	0.98522	0.98039	0.97561	0.97087	0.96618	0.96154	0.95694	0.95238	0.94787	0.94340	0.93897	0.93458
2	0.98030	0.97066	0.96117	0.95181	0.94260	0.93351	0.92456	0.91573	0.90703	0.89845	0.89000	0.88166	0.87344
3	0.97059	0.95632	0.94232	0.92860	0.91514	0.90194	0.88900	0.87630	0.86384	0.85161	0.83962	0.82785	0.81630
4	0.96098	0.94218	0.92385	0.90595	0.88849	0.87144	0.85480	0.83856	0.82270	0.80722	0.79209	0.77732	0.76290
5	0.95147	0.92826	0.90573	0.88385	0.86261	0.84197	0.82193	0.80245	0.78353	0.76513	0.74726	0.72988	0.71299
6	0.94205	0.91454	0.88797	0.86230	0.83748	0.81350	0.79031	0.76790	0.74622	0.72525	0.70496	0.68533	0.66634
7	0.93272	0.90103	0.87056	0.84126	0.81309	0.78599	0.75992	0.73483	0.71068	0.68744	0.66506	0.64351	0.62275
8	0.92348	0.88771	0.85349	0.82075	0.78941	0.75941	0.73069	0.70319	0.67684	0.65160	0.62741	0.60423	0.58201
9	0.91434	0.87459	0.83676	0.80073	0.76642	0.73373	0.70259	0.67290	0.64461	0.61763	0.59190	0.56735	0.54393
10	0.90529	0.86167	0.82035	0.78120	0.74409	0.70892	0.67556	0.64393	0.61391	0.58543	0.55840	0.53273	0.50835
11	0.89632	0.84893	0.80426	0.76214	0.72242	0.68495	0.64958	0.61620	0.58468	0.55491	0.52679	0.50021	0.47509
12	0.88745	0.83639	0.78849	0.74356	0.70138	0.66178	0.62460	0.58966	0.55684	0.52598	0.49697	0.46968	0.44401
13	0.87866	0.82403	0.77303	0.72542	0.68095	0.63940	0.60057	0.56427	0.53032	0.49856	0.46884	0.44102	0.41496
14	0.86996	0.81185	0.75787	0.70773	0.66112	0.61778	0.57748	0.53997	0.50507	0.47257	0.44230	0.41410	0.38782
15	0.86135	0.79985	0.74301	0.69046	0.64186	0.59689	0.55526	0.51672	0.48102	0.44793	0.41727	0.38883	0.36245
16	0.85282	0.78803	0.72845	0.67362	0.62317	0.57671	0.53391	0.49447	0.45811	0.42458	0.39365	0.36510	0.33874
17	0.84438	0.77638	0.71416	0.65719	0.60502	0.55720	0.51337	0.47318	0.43630	0.40245	0.37137	0.34281	0.31657
18	0.83602	0.76491	0.70016	0.64117	0.58739	0.53836	0.49363	0.45280	0.41552	0.38147	0.35034	0.32189	0.29586
19	0.82774	0.75361	0.68643	0.62553	0.57029	0.52015	0.47464	0.43330	0.39573	0.36158	0.33051	0.30224	0.27651
20	0.81954	0.74247	0.67297	0.61027	0.55368	0.50257	0.45639	0.41464	0.37689	0.34273	0.31181	0.28380	0.25842
21	0.81143	0.73150	0.65978	0.59539	0.53755	0.48557	0.43883	0.39679	0.35894	0.32486	0.29416	0.26648	0.24151
22	0.80340	0.72069	0.64684	0.58086	0.52189	0.46915	0.42196	0.37970	0.34185	0.30793	0.27751	0.25021	0.22571
23	0.79544	0.71003	0.63416	0.56670	0.50669	0.45328	0.40573	0.36335	0.32557	0.29187	0.26180	0.23494	0.21095
24	0.78757	0.69954	0.62172	0.55287	0.49193	0.43796	0.39012	0.34770	0.31007	0.27666	0.24698	0.22060	0.19715
25	0.77977	0.68920	0.60953	0.53939	0.47761	0.42315	0.37512	0.33273	0.29530	0.26223	0.23300	0.20714	0.18425
26	0.77205	0.67902	0.59758	0.52623	0.46369	0.40884	0.36069	0.31840	0.28124	0.24856	0.21981	0.19450	0.17220
27	0.76440	0.66898	0.58586	0.51340	0.45019	0.39501	0.34682	0.30469	0.26785	0.23560	0.20737	0.18262	0.16093
28	0.75684	0.65910	0.57437	0.50088	0.43708	0.38165	0.33348	0.29157	0.25509	0.22332	0.19563	0.17148	0.15040
29	0.74394	0.64936	0.56311	0.48866	0.42435	0.36875	0.32065	0.27901	0.24295	0.21168	0.18456	0.16101	0.14056
30	0.74192	0.63976	0.55207	0.47674	0.41199	0.35628	0.30832	0.26700	0.23138	0.20064	0.17411	0.15119	0.13137

(Continued)

Rate (%) Period (n)	7.5	8.0	8.5	9.0	9.5	10.0	10.5	11.0	11.5	12.0	12.5	13.0	13.5
1	0.93023	0.92593	0.92166	0.91743	0.91324	0.90909	0.90498	0.90090	0.89686	0.89286	0.88889	0.88496	0.88106
2	0.86533	0.85734	0.84946	0.84168	0.83401	0.82645	0.81898	0.81162	0.80436	0.79719	0.79012	0.78315	0.77626
3	0.80496	0.79383	0.78291	0.77218	0.76165	0.75131	0.74116	0.73119	0.72140	0.71178	0.70233	0.69305	0.68393
4	0.74880	0.73503	0.72157	0.70843	0.69557	0.68301	0.67073	0.65873	0.64699	0.63552	0.62430	0.61332	0.60258
5	0.69656	0.68058	0.66505	0.64993	0.63523	0.62092	0.60700	0.59345	0.58026	0.56743	0.55493	0.54276	0.53091
6	0.64796	0.63017	0.61294	0.59627	0.58012	0.56447	0.54932	0.53464	0.52042	0.50663	0.49327	0.48032	0.46776
7	0.60275	0.58349	0.56493	0.54703	0.52979	0.51316	0.49712	0.48166	0.46674	0.45235	0.43846	0.42506	0.41213
8	0.56070	0.54027	0.52067	0.50187	0.48382	0.46651	0.44989	0.43393	0.41860	0.40388	0.38974	0.37616	0.36311
9	0.52158	0.50025	0.47988	0.46043	0.44185	0.42410	0.40714	0.39093	0.37543	0.36061	0.34644	0.33288	0.31992
10	0.48519	0.46319	0.44229	0.42241	0.40351	0.38554	0.36845	0.35218	0.33671	0.32197	0.30795	0.29459	0.28187
11	0.45134	0.42888	0.40764	0.38753	0.36851	0.35049	0.33344	0.31728	0.30198	0.28748	0.27373	0.26070	0.24834
12	0.41985	0.39711	0.37570	0.35553	0.33653	0.31863	0.30175	0.28584	0.27083	0.25667	0.24332	0.23071	0.21880
13	0.39056	0.36770	0.34627	0.32618	0.30734	0.28966	0.27308	0.25751	0.24290	0.22917	0.21628	0.20416	0.19278
14	0.36331	0.34046	0.31914	0.29925	0.28067	0.26333	0.24713	0.23200	0.21785	0.20462	0.19225	0.18068	0.16985
15	0.33797	0.31524	0.29414	0.27454	0.25632	0.23939	0.22365	0.20900	0.19538	0.18270	0.17089	0.15989	0.14965
16	0.31439	0.29189	0.27110	0.25187	0.23408	0.21763	0.20240	0.18829	0.17523	0.16312	0.15190	0.14150	0.13185
17	0.29245	0.27027	0.24986	0.23107	0.21378	0.19784	0.18316	0.16963	0.15715	0.14564	0.13502	0.12522	0.11616
18	0.27205	0.25025	0.23028	0.21199	0.19523	0.17986	0.16576	0.15282	0.14095	0.13004	0.12002	0.11081	0.10235
19	0.25307	0.23171	0.21224	0.19449	0.17829	0.16351	0.15001	0.13768	0.12641	0.11611	0.10668	0.09806	0.09017
20	0.23541	0.21455	0.19562	0.17843	0.16282	0.14864	0.13575	0.12403	0.11337	0.10367	0.09483	0.08678	0.07945
21	0.21899	0.19866	0.18029	0.16370	0.14870	0.13513	0.12285	0.11174	0.10168	0.09256	0.08429	0.07680	0.07000
22	0.20371	0.18394	0.16617	0.15018	0.13580	0.12285	0.11118	0.10067	0.09119	0.08264	0.07493	0.06796	0.06167
23	0.18950	0.17032	0.15315	0.13778	0.12402	0.11168	0.10062	0.09069	0.08179	0.07379	0.06660	0.06014	0.05434
24	0.17628	0.15770	0.14115	0.12641	0.11326	0.10153	0.09106	0.08171	0.07335	0.06588	0.05920	0.05323	0.04787
25	0.16398	0.14602	0.13009	0.11597	0.10343	0.09230	0.08240	0.07361	0.06579	0.05882	0.05262	0.04710	0.04218
26	0.15254	0.13520	0.11990	0.10639	0.09446	0.08391	0.07457	0.06631	0.05900	0.05252	0.04678	0.04168	0.03716
27	0.14190	0.12519	0.11051	0.09761	0.08626	0.07628	0.06749	0.05974	0.05291	0.04689	0.04158	0.03689	0.03274
28	0.13200	0.11591	0.10185	0.08955	0.07878	0.06934	0.06107	0.05382	0.04746	0.04187	0.03696	0.03264	0.02885
29	0.12279	0.10733	0.09387	0.08215	0.07194	0.06304	0.05527	0.04849	0.04256	0.03738	0.03285	0.02889	0.02542
30	0.11422	0.09938	0.08652	0.07537	0.06570	0.05731	0.05002	0.04368	0.03817	0.03338	0.02920	0.02556	0.02239

Rate (%) Period (n)	14.0	14.5	15.0	16.0	17.0	18.0	19.0	20.0	22.0	24.0	26.0	28.0	30.0
1	0.87719	0.87336	0.86957	0.86207	0.85470	0.84746	0.84034	0.83333	0.81967	0.80645	0.79365	0.78125	0.76923
2	0.76947	0.76276	0.75614	0.74316	0.73051	0.71818	0.70616	0.69444	0.67186	0.65036	0.62988	0.61035	0.59172
3	0.67497	0.66617	0.65752	0.64066	0.62437	0.60863	0.59342	0.57870	0.55071	0.52449	0.49991	0.47684	0.45517
4	0.59208	0.58181	0.57175	0.55229	0.53365	0.51579	0.49867	0.48225	0.45140	0.42297	0.39675	0.37253	0.35013
5	0.51937	0.50813	0.49718	0.47611	0.45611	0.43711	0.41905	0.40188	0.37000	0.34111	0.31488	0.29104	0.26933
6	0.45559	0.44378	0.43233	0.41044	0.38984	0.37043	0.35214	0.33490	0.30328	0.27509	0.24991	0.22737	0.20718
7	0.39964	0.38758	0.37594	0.35383	0.33320	0.31392	0.29592	0.27908	0.24859	0.22184	0.19834	0.17764	0.15937
8	0.35056	0.33850	0.32690	0.30503	0.28478	0.26604	0.24867	0.23257	0.20376	0.17891	0.15741	0.13878	0.12259
9	0.30751	0.29563	0.28426	0.26295	0.24340	0.22546	0.20897	0.19381	0.16702	0.14428	0.12493	0.10842	0.09430
10	0.26974	0.25819	0.24718	0.22668	0.20804	0.19106	0.17560	0.16151	0.13690	0.11635	0.09915	0.08470	0.07254
11	0.23662	0.22550	0.21494	0.19542	0.17781	0.16192	0.14757	0.13459	0.11221	0.09383	0.07869	0.06617	0.05580
12	0.20756	0.19694	0.18691	0.16846	0.15197	0.13722	0.12400	0.11216	0.09198	0.07567	0.06245	0.05170	0.04292
13	0.18207	0.17200	0.16253	0.14523	0.12989	0.11629	0.10421	0.09346	0.07539	0.06103	0.04957	0.04039	0.03302
14	0.15971	0.15022	0.14133	0.12520	0.11102	0.09855	0.08757	0.07789	0.06180	0.04921	0.03934	0.03155	0.02540
15	0.14010	0.13120	0.12289	0.10793	0.09489	0.08352	0.07359	0.06491	0.05065	0.03969	0.03122	0.02465	0.01954
16	0.12289	0.11458	0.10686	0.09304	0.08110	0.07078	0.06184	0.05409	0.04152	0.03201	0.02478	0.01926	0.01503
17	0.10780	0.10007	0.09293	0.08021	0.06932	0.05998	0.05196	0.04507	0.03403	0.02581	0.01967	0.01505	0.01156
18	0.09456	0.08740	0.08080	0.06914	0.05925	0.05083	0.04367	0.03756	0.02789	0.02082	0.01561	0.01175	0.00889
19	0.08295	0.07633	0.07027	0.05961	0.05064	0.04308	0.03670	0.03130	0.02286	0.01679	0.01239	0.00918	0.00684
20	0.07276	0.06666	0.06110	0.05139	0.04328	0.03651	0.03084	0.02608	0.01874	0.01354	0.00983	0.00717	0.00526
21	0.06383	0.05822	0.05313	0.04430	0.03699	0.03094	0.02591	0.02174	0.01536	0.01092	0.00780	0.00561	0.00405
22	0.05599	0.05085	0.04620	0.03819	0.03162	0.02622	0.02178	0.01811	0.01259	0.00880	0.00619	0.00438	0.00311
23	0.04911	0.04441	0.04017	0.03292	0.02702	0.02222	0.01830	0.01509	0.01032	0.00710	0.00491	0.00342	0.00239
24	0.04308	0.03879	0.03493	0.02838	0.02310	0.01883	0.01538	0.01258	0.00846	0.00573	0.00390	0.00267	0.00184
25	0.03779	0.03387	0.03038	0.02447	0.01974	0.01596	0.01292	0.01048	0.00693	0.00462	0.00310	0.00209	0.00142
26	0.03315	0.02958	0.02642	0.02109	0.01687	0.01352	0.01086	0.00874	0.00568	0.00372	0.00246	0.00163	0.00109
27	0.02908	0.02584	0.02297	0.01818	0.01442	0.01146	0.00912	0.00728	0.00466	0.00300	0.00195	0.00127	0.00084
28	0.02551	0.02257	0.01997	0.01567	0.01233	0.00971	0.00767	0.00607	0.00382	0.00242	0.00155	0.00100	0.00065
29	0.02237	0.01971	0.01737	0.01351	0.01053	0.00823	0.00644	0.00506	0.00313	0.00195	0.00123	0.00078	0.00050
30	0.01963	0.01721	0.01510	0.01165	0.00900	0.00697	0.00541	0.00421	0.00257	0.00158	0.00097	0.00061	0.00038

Table A

Table B Present value of an annuity of £1: $(1/R)(1 - (1/(1 + R))^n)$

Rate (%) / Period (n)	1.0	1.5	2.0	2.5	3.0	3.5	4.0	4.5	5.0	5.5	6.0	6.5	7.0
1	0.99009	0.98523	0.98039	0.97561	0.97087	0.96618	0.96154	0.95694	0.95238	0.94787	0.94339	0.93897	0.93458
2	1.97039	1.95590	1.94156	1.92743	1.91347	1.89970	1.88609	1.87267	1.85941	1.84632	1.83339	1.82063	1.80802
3	2.94098	2.91223	2.88388	2.85603	2.82861	2.80164	2.77509	2.74897	2.72325	2.69794	2.67301	2.64848	2.62431
4	3.90196	3.85442	3.80774	3.76198	3.71710	3.67309	3.62989	3.58753	3.54595	3.50516	3.46510	3.42580	3.38721
5	4.85342	4.78269	4.71346	4.64584	4.57971	4.51507	4.45182	4.38998	4.32947	4.27029	4.21236	4.15568	4.10019
6	5.79546	5.69723	5.60144	5.50813	5.41719	5.32856	5.24213	5.15788	5.07569	4.99554	4.91732	4.84102	4.76653
7	6.72816	6.59828	6.47199	6.34940	6.23028	6.11456	6.00205	5.89270	5.78637	5.68297	5.58237	5.48452	5.38929
8	7.65165	7.48599	7.32549	7.17016	7.01969	6.87397	6.73274	6.59589	6.46321	6.33457	6.20978	6.08876	5.97129
9	8.56599	8.36058	8.16225	7.97089	7.78611	7.60770	7.43533	7.26879	7.10782	6.95220	6.80168	6.65611	6.51523
10	9.47126	9.22227	8.98260	8.75208	8.53020	8.31662	8.11090	7.91272	7.72173	7.53763	7.36008	7.18884	7.02358
11	10.36758	10.07121	9.78686	9.51423	9.25262	9.00157	8.76047	8.52892	8.30641	8.09254	7.88686	7.68905	7.49867
12	11.25505	10.90760	10.57536	10.25779	9.95401	9.66335	9.38507	9.11858	8.86325	8.61853	8.38383	8.15873	7.94268
13	12.13369	11.73164	11.34839	10.98322	10.63495	10.30276	9.98564	9.68286	9.39357	9.11709	8.85267	8.59975	8.35765
14	13.00366	12.54349	12.10626	11.69094	11.29607	10.92054	10.56312	10.22283	9.89864	9.58966	9.29497	9.01385	8.74546
15	13.86501	13.34335	12.84928	12.38140	11.93794	11.51743	11.11838	10.73955	10.37966	10.03759	9.71224	9.40267	9.10791
16	14.71783	14.13139	13.57773	13.05503	12.56110	12.09414	11.65229	11.23402	10.83777	10.46217	10.10588	9.76777	9.44664
17	15.56220	14.90777	14.29189	13.71223	13.16612	12.65134	12.16567	11.70719	11.27406	10.86462	10.47725	10.11058	9.76322
18	16.39822	15.67270	14.99205	14.35340	13.75351	13.18971	12.65929	12.15999	11.68958	11.24608	10.82759	10.43247	10.05908
19	17.22596	16.42632	15.67848	14.97892	14.32380	13.70986	13.13393	12.59330	12.08532	11.60766	11.15811	10.73472	10.33559
20	18.04551	17.16878	16.35146	15.58920	14.87747	14.21243	13.59032	13.00794	12.46221	11.95039	11.46991	11.01851	10.59401
21	18.85693	17.90029	17.01123	16.18459	15.41502	14.69800	14.02916	13.40473	12.82115	12.27525	11.76406	11.28499	10.83552
22	19.66032	18.62098	17.65807	16.76545	15.93691	15.16715	14.45111	13.78443	13.16300	12.58318	12.04157	11.53520	11.06124
23	20.45577	19.33103	18.29222	17.33214	16.44361	15.62044	14.85684	14.14778	13.48857	12.87505	12.30337	11.77014	11.27218
24	21.24332	20.03057	18.91395	17.88502	16.93554	16.05839	15.24696	14.49548	13.79864	13.15171	12.55035	11.99074	11.46933
25	22.02309	20.71977	19.52348	18.42442	17.41315	16.48154	15.62208	14.82821	14.09394	13.41394	12.78335	12.19788	11.65358
26	22.79514	21.39881	20.12106	18.95065	17.87684	16.89038	15.98277	15.14662	14.37518	13.66250	13.00316	12.39238	11.82577
27	23.55955	22.06780	20.70692	19.46405	18.32703	17.28539	16.32958	15.45130	14.64303	13.89811	13.21052	12.57500	11.98671
28	24.31637	22.72690	21.28130	19.96493	18.76411	17.66705	16.66306	15.74288	14.89812	14.12143	13.40615	12.74648	12.13711
29	25.06572	23.37627	21.84441	20.45359	19.18845	18.03579	16.98371	16.02189	15.14107	14.33311	13.59071	12.90749	12.27767
30	25.80764	24.01602	22.39648	20.93033	19.60044	18.39207	17.29203	16.28889	15.37245	14.53375	13.76482	13.05868	12.40904

Rate (%) Period (n)	7.5	8.0	8.5	9.0	9.5	10.0	10.5	11.0	11.5	12.0	12.5	13.0	13.5
1	0.93023	0.92593	0.92166	0.91743	0.91324	0.90909	0.90498	0.90090	0.89686	0.89286	0.88889	0.88496	0.88106
2	1.79557	1.78326	1.77111	1.75911	1.74725	1.73554	1.72396	1.71252	1.70122	1.69005	1.67901	1.66810	1.65732
3	2.60053	2.57709	2.55402	2.53129	2.50891	2.48685	2.46512	2.44371	2.42262	2.40183	2.38134	2.36115	2.34125
4	3.34933	3.31212	3.27560	3.23972	3.20448	3.16986	3.13586	3.10244	3.06962	3.03735	3.00564	2.97447	2.94383
5	4.04589	3.99271	3.94064	3.88965	3.83971	3.79078	3.74286	3.69589	3.64988	3.60478	3.56057	3.51723	3.47474
6	4.69385	4.62288	4.55359	4.48592	4.41983	4.35526	4.29218	4.23054	4.17030	4.11141	4.05384	3.99755	3.94250
7	5.29660	5.20636	5.11852	5.03295	4.94961	4.86842	4.78930	4.71219	4.63704	4.56376	4.49230	4.42261	4.35463
8	5.85731	5.74663	5.63919	5.53482	5.43344	5.33492	5.23919	5.14612	5.05564	4.96764	4.88205	4.79877	4.71774
9	6.37889	6.24688	6.11907	5.99524	5.87529	5.75902	5.64632	5.53704	5.43107	5.32825	5.22848	5.13166	5.03765
10	6.86408	6.71007	6.56135	6.41766	6.27880	6.14456	6.01477	5.88923	5.76777	5.65023	5.53643	5.42625	5.31952
11	7.31543	7.13896	6.96899	6.80519	6.64731	6.49506	6.34821	6.20651	6.06975	5.93770	5.81016	5.68694	5.56786
12	7.73528	7.53607	7.34469	7.16072	6.98384	6.81369	6.64996	6.49235	6.34058	6.19438	6.05348	5.91765	5.78666
13	8.12584	7.90377	7.69096	7.48690	7.29118	7.10335	6.92304	6.74987	6.58348	6.42355	6.26976	6.12181	5.97943
14	8.48816	8.24423	8.01010	7.78615	7.57185	7.36668	7.17018	6.98186	6.80133	6.62817	6.46201	6.30249	6.14928
15	8.82712	8.55947	8.30424	8.06069	7.82818	7.60608	7.39382	7.19087	6.99671	6.81087	6.63289	6.46238	6.29893
16	9.14151	8.85136	8.57534	8.31256	8.06226	7.82371	7.59622	7.37916	7.17194	6.97399	6.78479	6.60388	6.43077
17	9.43396	9.12163	8.82520	8.54363	8.27604	8.02155	7.77939	7.54879	7.32909	7.11963	6.91982	6.72909	6.54694
18	9.70601	9.37188	9.05548	8.75562	8.47127	8.20141	7.94514	7.70161	7.47004	7.24967	7.03984	6.83991	6.64928
19	9.95908	9.60359	9.26772	8.95011	8.64956	8.36492	8.09515	7.83929	7.59645	7.36578	7.14652	6.93797	6.73946
20	10.19450	9.81814	9.46334	9.12854	8.81238	8.51356	8.23091	7.96333	7.70982	7.46944	7.24135	7.02475	6.81890
21	10.41348	10.01680	9.64363	9.29224	8.96108	8.64869	8.35376	8.07507	7.81150	7.56200	7.32565	7.10155	6.88890
22	10.61719	10.20074	9.80980	9.44242	9.09688	8.77154	8.46494	8.17574	7.90269	7.64465	7.40058	7.16951	6.95057
23	10.80669	10.37105	9.96295	9.58020	9.22089	8.88322	8.56556	8.26643	7.98447	7.71843	7.46718	7.22966	7.00491
24	10.98297	10.52875	10.10410	9.70661	9.33415	8.98474	8.65662	8.34813	8.05782	7.78432	7.52638	7.28288	7.05279
25	11.14695	10.67477	10.23419	9.82258	9.43758	9.07704	8.73902	8.42174	8.12361	7.84314	7.57901	7.32999	7.09497
26	11.29949	10.80997	10.35410	9.92897	9.53204	9.16094	8.81359	8.48806	8.18261	7.89566	7.62578	7.37167	7.13213
27	11.44138	10.93516	10.46460	10.02658	9.61830	9.23722	8.88108	8.54780	8.23552	7.94255	7.66736	7.40856	7.16487
28	11.57338	11.05100	10.56646	10.11613	9.69708	9.30657	8.94215	8.60162	8.28298	7.98442	7.70432	7.44120	7.19372
29	11.69617	11.15840	10.66033	10.19828	9.76902	9.36960	8.99742	8.65011	8.32554	8.02181	7.73717	7.47009	7.21914
30	11.81039	11.25778	10.74685	10.27365	9.83472	9.42691	9.04744	8.69379	8.36372	8.05518	7.76638	7.49565	7.24153

(Continued)

Rate (%) / Period (n)	14.0	14.5	15.0	16.0	17.0	18.0	19.0	20.0	22.0	24.0	26.0	28.0	30.0
1	0.87719	0.87336	0.86957	0.86207	0.85470	0.84746	0.84034	0.83333	0.81967	0.80645	0.79365	0.78125	0.76923
2	1.64666	1.63612	1.62571	1.60523	1.58521	1.56564	1.54650	1.52778	1.49153	1.45682	1.42353	1.39160	1.36095
3	2.32163	2.30229	2.28323	2.24589	2.20959	2.17427	2.13992	2.10648	2.04224	1.98130	1.92344	1.86844	1.81611
4	2.91371	2.88410	2.85498	2.79818	2.74324	2.69006	2.63859	2.58874	2.49364	2.40428	2.32019	2.24097	2.16624
5	3.43308	3.39222	3.35216	3.27429	3.19935	3.12717	3.05763	2.99061	2.86364	2.74538	2.63507	2.53201	2.43557
6	3.88867	3.83600	3.78448	3.68474	3.58919	3.49760	3.40978	3.32551	3.16692	3.02047	2.88498	2.75938	2.64275
7	4.28831	4.22358	4.16042	4.03857	3.92238	3.81153	3.70570	3.60459	3.41551	3.24332	3.08232	2.93702	2.80211
8	4.63887	4.56208	4.48732	4.34359	4.20716	4.07757	3.95437	3.83716	3.61927	3.42122	3.24073	3.07579	2.92470
9	4.94637	4.85771	4.77159	4.60654	4.45057	4.30302	4.16333	4.03097	3.78628	3.56550	3.36566	3.18421	3.01900
10	5.21612	5.11591	5.01877	4.83323	4.65860	4.49409	4.33893	4.19247	3.92318	3.68186	3.46481	3.26892	3.09154
11	5.45273	5.34140	5.23371	5.02864	4.83641	4.65601	4.48650	4.32706	4.03540	3.77569	3.54350	3.33509	3.14734
12	5.66029	5.53834	5.42062	5.19711	4.98839	4.79323	4.61050	4.43922	4.12737	3.85136	3.60595	3.38679	3.19026
13	5.84236	5.71034	5.58315	5.34233	5.11828	4.90951	4.71471	4.53268	4.20277	3.91239	3.65552	3.42718	3.22328
14	6.00207	5.86056	5.72448	5.46753	5.22930	5.00806	4.80228	4.61057	4.26456	3.96160	3.69485	3.45873	3.24867
15	6.14217	5.99176	5.84737	5.57546	5.32419	5.09158	4.87586	4.67547	4.31522	4.00129	3.72607	3.48339	3.26821
16	6.26506	6.10634	5.95424	5.66850	5.40529	5.16235	4.93770	4.72956	4.35673	4.03330	3.75085	3.50265	3.28324
17	6.37286	6.20641	6.04716	5.74870	5.47461	5.22233	4.98966	4.77463	4.39077	4.05911	3.77052	3.51769	3.29480
18	6.46742	6.29381	6.12797	5.81785	5.53385	5.27316	5.03333	4.81220	4.41866	4.07993	3.78613	3.52945	3.30369
19	6.55037	6.37014	6.19823	5.87746	5.58446	5.31624	5.07003	4.84350	4.44152	4.09672	3.79851	3.53863	3.31053
20	6.62313	6.43680	6.25933	5.92884	5.62777	5.35275	5.10086	4.86958	4.46027	4.11026	3.80834	3.54581	3.31579
21	6.68696	6.49502	6.31246	5.97314	5.66476	5.38368	5.12677	4.89132	4.47563	4.12117	3.81615	3.55141	3.31984
22	6.74295	6.54587	6.35866	6.01133	5.69638	5.40990	5.14855	4.90943	4.48822	4.12998	3.82234	3.55579	3.32295
23	6.79206	6.59028	6.39884	6.04425	5.72340	5.43212	5.16685	4.92453	4.49854	4.13708	3.82725	3.55921	3.32535
24	6.83514	6.62907	6.43377	6.07263	5.74649	5.45095	5.18223	4.93710	4.50700	4.14281	3.83115	3.56188	3.32719
25	6.87293	6.66294	6.46415	6.09709	5.76623	5.46691	5.19515	4.94759	4.51393	4.14742	3.83425	3.56397	3.32861
26	6.90608	6.69252	6.49056	6.11818	5.78311	5.48043	5.20601	4.95632	4.51962	4.15115	3.83670	3.56560	3.32970
27	6.93516	6.71836	6.51353	6.13636	5.79753	5.49189	5.21513	4.96360	4.52428	4.15415	3.83865	3.56688	3.33054
28	6.96066	6.74093	6.53351	6.15204	5.80985	5.50160	5.22280	4.96967	4.52810	4.15657	3.84020	3.56787	3.33118
29	6.98304	6.76063	6.55088	6.16555	5.82039	5.50983	5.22924	4.97472	4.53123	4.15853	3.84143	3.56865	3.33168
30	7.00267	6.77785	6.56598	6.17720	5.82939	5.51681	5.23466	4.97894	4.53379	4.16010	3.84241	3.56926	3.33206

Project Evaluation and the Monitoring of Performance

Hawkins, C. J. and Pearce, D. W (1971) *Capital Investment Appraisal*, Basingstoke: Macmillan.

Lumby, S. (1991) *Investment Appraisal and Financial Decisions*, London: International Thomson Business Press.

Sangster, A. (1993) 'Capital Investment Appraisal Techniques: A Survey of Current Usage', *Journal of Business Finance and Accounting* 20(3): 307–32.

INDEX